OSCAR FABER

his work, his firm, & afterwards

John Faber

QUILLER PRESS

First published 1989 by
Quiller Press Limited
46 Lillie Road, London SW6 1TN

Copyright © John Faber, 1989

ISBN 1 870948 17 3

All rights reserved. No part of this book may be reproduced or transmitted, in any form or by any means, without permission of the publishers.

Design and production in association with Book Production Consultants, 47 Norfolk Street, Cambridge.

Typeset by Witwoll Ltd, Southport.

Printed and bound by Oxford University Press.

Contents

Preface v
1 The Origins 1
2 Earlier Career 7
3 Jim Vaughan and Rob Kell 25
4 The Heyday of Romney House 43
5 The Second World War Period 59
6 Into Partnership 73
7 After Oscar Faber's Death 93

Preface

Ten years ago I wrote a somewhat different book, about the firm of Oscar Faber & Partners which was, in effect, a second generation progeny created forty years ago. That old firm, which had been born of the strength of the 'sole practice' my father – Oscar Faber – had founded in 1921, and in which I worked for many years, no longer exists in the style it then was: it operates now as a limited liability company. My earlier book which was circulated privately to a number of friends, was never published for fear of affronting the sensibilities of one or two of the earlier seniors then remaining within the firm. Those considerations no long apply; and it seems timely to offer the present story which has, as its main emphasis, the work of Oscar Faber – the man – together with his closest colleagues who supported him, and the way things continued over the period shortly following his death in 1956.

The old firm of Oscar Faber & Partners was built up from the energy and brilliance of three men. Without the personality of Oscar Faber there would have been no firm at all; without Stanley Vaughan (Jim) there would have been inadequate academic patience to set the high standard of structural detail that was achieved; and without John Robert Kell (Rob) the build-up of knowledge and practical sense in mechanical and electrical work would never have got off the ground. These three were the pioneers of the firm in the special style and character it developed: all three were needed; all three benefitted from the mutual experience. Each had the highest standards of integrity; otherwise, in many respects, they were very different people. Vaughan worked with Faber from 1920 and throughout; Kell did the same from 1925.

Naturally I was close enough to my father to have a fair insight into what went on with him over much of his working life; and the stories he used to tell of his earlier days, and all his records, provide a fund of information. Vaughan died in 1979 – twenty-three years after my father – and, for various purposes, had been giving me over those years much material about the early days of their work together – all in written form. Kell was still alive, vigorous and gifted with a fine memory whilst I was writing the forerunner of the present book. He helped me with many conversations at home, and wrote me numerous letters each of ten or twenty pages. Kell died later in 1983.

In addition to all this information, I have had help from many old friends and colleagues in the 'family firm's affairs – too many to make it appropriate or desirable to make individual acknowledgements, but all greatly appreciated. And of course I have had access to the libraries of all the great engineering institutions, as also to the archives of the old firm where the librarian, Harold Smith, gave me continuous help. Much enthusiasm, too, has come from my wife Denise whose patience has been a boon as the pieces of the story have come together and fallen into some sort of sensible shape.

It has been a problem to know how many people's names should be included in the book. There are hundreds that could have been chosen – friends, members of the firm, clients, architects, engineers, quantity surveyors, and those of other allied professions. The least number has seemed safest: some that are omitted may wish they were in; some that are in may wish they were not! The same question arises on how many engineering projects to mention or describe.

The book is no catalogue of all the work that Oscar Faber did, nor of all the researches he and his firm carried out, nor of all the papers and books written and published; nor does it follow rigidly any chronological order. Looking back over the affairs within and surrounding the man and his work, with all its many facets, one can visualise a sort of four-dimensional shape through which certain threads of continuity run in various directions; and the aim in writing the book has been to follow a few of these in the hope they may provide, as light reading, some pleasure to surviving contemporaries and to others who may be interested to know a little more of the man who founded and created what became one of the leading firms of Consulting Engineers in Britain.

John Faber
Old Welwyn, Herts
1988

1

The Origins

In 1971 the firm of Oscar Faber & Partners celebrated its fiftieth anniversary. To appreciate what had been achieved and from what beginnings it had come, one needs to go back and remember the mood of things fifty years before.

Following the Great War of 1914-18, Britain had gone through a short-lived economic boom, and then smack into the Great Depression starting at the end of 1920. By the summer of 1919, the greater part of the army had been demobilised; and there was overall confidence that British goods, if produced again quickly, would find a healthy overseas market, and Britain would be back to the strong position it had enjoyed before the War. Wartime controls were removed, capital investment went wild, and prices and wages raced upwards. Everything seemed to be going fine. But alas Britain had priced herself out of business in a market that was not yet in a position to buy anything. Inflation was upon us.

The boom came to an end in the winter of 1920-21. The economic and social consequences were disastrous: Government spending was abruptly cut, and 2 million *men* were on the dole – in those days a most meagre provision. This was followed by a general fall in wages in all industries across the country. Taxation reached the peak of that time. Interest rates had been hiked up. Such a situation could not have had a more discouraging effect on anyone who wanted to start a new business.

Yet, in 1921, Oscar Faber, a daring and energetic young man, eight years married and with wife and three children to support, decided to chance his arm working on his own account as an independent consulting engineer. At the age of thirty-five, with £2000 capital, he put up his plate at a small private house at 5 South Street, near Finsbury Circus, in the City of London, where he rented three rooms on the second floor. The stairs up were narrow and creaky, and the lavatory was squeezed in on the half-landing. The only heating in the smaller of the three rooms was by Bunsen burners standing on the desk tops. The initial staff consisted of two engineers, one office junior, and a typist. It was this small nucleus that was to grow and later become the practice known as Oscar Faber & Partners.

But what were the origins of this vital man who pulled himself up with scholarship awards through school and university, and who by the age of thirty-eight had in his hand the personal appointment of consulting engineer for the new Bank of England, including the whole of the superstructure work, three levels of basement extending right up against the adjoining streets in the busiest part of the City of London, and who conceived a self-sufficient services system with its own electricity-generating plant – the exhaust energy being conserved and converted for use to meet heating needs – a water-supply system fed from pump-assisted artesian wells below, and the whole of the normal environmental services including power, lighting, lifts, air-conditioning and so on?

In addition to his great competence as an engineer, Oscar Faber had a remarkable breadth of talent outside his working responsibilities. Following *The Times* formal obituary in May 1956 listing a number of his professional achievements, his friend, Richard Charques – then on *The Times* staff – added a footnote in the form of a spontaneous expression, part of which read:

> "It is hard to realise that Oscar Faber has gone. Nobody had more abundant life, nobody appeared to possess such inexhaustible energy. He was a prodigy of a man in his vitality, his zest for living, his capacity for work, his appetite for recreation. Big and heavy of frame, splendidly untidy in appearance, his eyes very blue and clear, bushy grey brows jutting out over flaming cheeks, he had always something of the air of a still untamed Viking. The distinction of the man was unmistakable. Character in him, as character often does, ran to eccentricity; he would confess his foibles and failings with a small boy's artful candour. With all his idiosyncrasies of behaviour he was a very lovable person.
>
> "Oscar drove himself hard in his work; he had more than a little of the Carlylean religion of work. But he was also astonishingly versatile. He was a watercolour painter of unpretentious but real ability and painted enthusiastically on his travels. He adored Elgar and sang in a still attractive tenor voice. He gardened furiously. He played golf with erratic energy. An ex-Fabian Conservative, his mind was rational and extraordinarily lucid. He would pursue an argument in the quietest tone of voice, steadily lowering it as he warmed to his conclusions until he became almost inaudible. A schoolboy's sense of fun and adventure lurked always in him."

Oscar Faber had been born in London in 1886. He was British through and through, but nevertheless very proud of his Danish ancestry which can be traced back through many generations to a community of well-to-do farmers. The Danes all love, and always have loved, the beauty and culture of their small homeland: in this they have a strong sense of close-knit nationalism. Nevertheless, as history records – not always too kindly! – they are natural adventurers and never free from the urge to travel in search of broader experience and in pursuit of commercial prize. The Faber family has been no exception; and indeed the name itself, taken from the Latin by one Nicholai (1722–81), was to set a challenge on a deliberate course towards professionalism.

Nicholai Faber was a farmer/forester at Odense in the central Danish island of Fyn. Of his sons, one became a war consultant, another a printer, and the third, Rasmus Faber – not quite as expected – one of the early Copenhagen brewers. One of Rasmus's sons, Nicholai the Second, perhaps disapproving of his father's involvement in the froth of Danish lager, turned to the Church and became a bishop; he studied music and excelled in it: his professional work included the writing of many books to do with the Church and to help raise the standard and facilities in Denmark for education. One of the bishop's sons, well named Christian, and no doubt influenced by his father's writings, took a job as a grammar-school teacher: later he was to become a Member of the Danish Parliament.

Christian Faber (1822–83) was Oscar Faber's grandfather. He married Bertha Bruun Muus (Brown Mouse), the second of thirteen children of Marie Bruun and Elias Muus, the latter a farm merchant. Christian took Bertha back to Odense, where she reared a quite remarkable family of six, of which four were sons, Harald, Knud, Svend and Erik, all professional. The youngest, Erik was a doctor: before him was Svend, an electrical engineer, graduated in 1893 at the School of Electrical and Mechanical Engineering in London, held posts in London, Nurenburg, Paris and Berlin, including Director of the Copenhagen Tramway Co. where he was responsible for the electrification of the whole of the city's tramway system. Older brother, Knud, became a leading surgeon in Denmark, having earlier in his career researched Tetanus and produced the toxin; became Professor of Clinical Medicine at the age of thirty-four, and wrote many books and lectured widely in Denmark, Sweden, England, Germany and Iceland.

But it was really Harald, the eldest son, who had set the pace. Harald Faber (1856–1944) was Oscar Faber's father. Born within the farming community of Odense, but having no special enthusiasm for hens, pigs or cows, he had studied natural sciences, graduating at Copenhagen University in 1881. His first job was with a sugar factory in Odense, but he was quickly off to the USA to take up the position of chemist to the Pennsylvania Salt Manufacturing Co., and then to London to be chemist to the Dairy Supply Co. In 1888 he was appointed Agricultural Commissioner for Denmark, a most important commercial post for that country, then almost entirely reliant on its agricultural trade; so in a sense he was now back to hens, pigs and cows again. He was given the London office – Britain being Denmark's major customer of dairy products – and had consultancy responsibilities covering trade with Belgium and France too. At the time of his appointment there was much resistance in Britain to the import of Danish products, and many years had to be spent in countering this prejudice. As an early exercise in logo, he designed the Lurmaerket sign. Harald held the post of Agricultural Commissioner for forty-three years until his retirement in 1931. Over this period he wrote many books to do with his work. The Danish Biological Dictionary says, "No other person has had such a great influence on the sale of Danish Agricultural Products on the English market."

In 1885 Harald Faber made a return visit to Copenhagen to marry Cecilie Bentzien, who came back with him to London. Oscar was born a year later, the first of six children – three boys and three girls. One of Oscar's brothers, Erik, six years his junior, was also to become a notable consulting engineer, setting up his practice in Hong Kong in 1928. Erik Faber specialised in structural engineering, and will perhaps be remembered best for his work on the Hong Kong Ocean Terminal.

By the age of eleven, young Oscar had worked his way to school as a Scholarship boy at St. Dunstan's College at Catford in South London. His achievements there were sound and broadly based. He was a Committee Member of the Literary and Debating Club, and also the Natural History and Archaeological Club; he became Secretary of the Union Society; he was Chairman of the Camera Club; he was awarded his colours for lacrosse and rugby football. From his first year until he left, he sang solo at nearly every school concert, having a yen for humour over the mysteries of Japan and China, with songs like 'Tit-willow', 'Chin Chin Chinaman', 'Chinee Sojee Man' and 'Me Gette out Quick'. He also made his mark at shooting matches with rifles using a Morris tube.

In his last year (1903) he was Head of the School, Editor of the Chronicle, and took prizes for Maths, Science, Engineering, French, Reading and Drawing. He also won for himself the most coveted scholarship available to the Central Technical College (now City and Guilds College) being the Clothworkers Scholarship, awarded to the student having the highest marking in the Matriculation Examination – that year 175 students had applied. The Dean of the College, Professor W. C. Unwin – subsequently to become a special friend and *confrère* – took the trouble to write in his own hand to Oscar at the school, informing him of this achievement and congratulating him. The example of Professor Unwin's realistic analytical approach to all matters of engineering, and concise unambiguous use of the English language, were to make a great mark on the young student who was shortly to come under his influence.

At the City and Guilds, part of Imperial College of London University, Faber chose the course in electrical engineering. In this he was no doubt influenced by the progress of his Uncle Svend, only nineteen years his senior; but the choice was far-sighted for a young man in Britain at that time. England had developed earlier and more rapidly than the United States and Europe, and had stolen an economic march by the development of her coal potential to provide steam-power and to produce gas for both lighting and industrial power. A great proportion of industry still drove its machinery by ropes and belts from shafts driven from their own engines. Why should all this change? The crippling provisions of the 1882 Electric Lighting Act had done everything possible to prevent it. At the turn of the century, lighting by electricity was still experimental and much regarded as a luxury. Supply systems were unreliable, and varied as to voltage. More D. C. was provided than A.C. In 1896 a mere 30 million kWh of electricity was sold throughout the whole UK – less than a kilowatt per person per year. The comparable figure in 1986 was about 250,000 million.

Two years later, in 1905, Faber graduated in electrical engineering, by which time his active mind had spotted the opportunities that could come from a new construction technique that was becoming known as ferro-concrete or reinforced-concrete. The practice of strengthening concrete by embedding iron beams or bars or ropes in it had been going on through the nineteenth century, but all on a rule-of-thumb basis with very little theoretical appreciation. Early pioneers were seeking to unravel the analysis of this composite material, perhaps notably Neumann in 1890, Coignet in 1894, and Considère in 1895; but by 1905 there was emerging little more than the first bones of any real understanding. Oscar Faber knew he would dearly love to be involved in this study; and so, for a post-graduate year, he transferred to the Civil and Mechanical Department, where he took reinforced-concrete as his research subject.

Throughout his period at college, Mr. Faber, as he then was, took an active part in the affairs of the Engineering Society, speaking at many of the meetings. Despite having transferred from the Electrical Department, he wrote and presented a paper in 1906 entitled Turbo-Generators, and for the following day had organised a party of students to visit the power-station at Lots Road, Chelsea, where a guided tour was laid on to witness such machines being installed and test run. That same year, he graduated in civil and mechanical engineering.

Years later, in 1944, Dr. Oscar Faber was installed as President of the Engineering Society of the City and Guilds. His address that day was largely to do with foundation problems, and drew an audience of unprecedented size – 160 members and 30 visitors. The same year he donated £200 to the Engineering Society for a Faber Prize to be awarded each year for the best paper written and presented before the Society. The term 'Faber Prizeman' is still included in the record of the student's academic career.

As a further aside one might note that during the first decade of this century very few Danish civil engineers were resident in the UK. But between 1910 and 1921 the numbers increased to such an extent it was decided to form a Society of Danish Civil Engineers in Great Britain and Ireland, – based in London. This was immediately recognised by the Dansk Ingenior Forening in Copenhagen, and a close working link between the two has remained. At the first meeting of the Society in 1922, Harald Faber was elected as its Chairman, a position he held until 1931. By then he was seventy-five and handing over his task as Agricultural Commissioner: and he and his wife were to return to Copenhagen, where they lived their lives out together almost another fifteen years. Right to the last, Harald involved himself personally at the University in a geological research programme of his own initiation. In the period of Harald's chairmanship, the Society of Danish Civil Engineers grew in numbers to over fifty, including names like Bierrum, Christiani, Holst, Kier, Larsen, Lind, Theilmann. Oscar Faber did not join until the year after his father had stood down; this was a pity and may have been a little churlish of him.

2

Earlier Career

Most great men are a product of their own qualities and the associations they have with other people, and all the fruits that derive from these. Oscar Faber was no exception. His life became his work, and his work became his firm; and in this environment he was forever in the closest touch with his many colleagues – almost telepathic, one might say – over considerable concentrated spells. In this way the energy of his mind was spread down through his team, whilst at the same time he could assimilate support-contribution coming back from those around. Thus, to portray the man, I have sometimes found it necessary here to pause and elaborate the detail of his colleagues, being, as they were, the backcloth to my principal character. Indeed because of the closeness of all these relationships, I have, at times, quoted freely from these other men's recollections wherever I have felt their words could not be bettered. In the general perspectives which follow, an attempt has been made to pick out a few of the principal markers that highlight the various facets of Oscar Faber's personality and the undoubted genius of his engineering.

Jim Vaughan, who was closer to him for more of his developing years than anyone else, wrote in a personal letter to me in 1968:

> "All the steps through his life appear to fit in with a definite 'career plan'. Whether such a plan was ever consciously set down by Dr. Faber to form guidelines to the development of his career, or whether this remained in his subconscious mind, his career conformed with remarkable consistency with such a plan, and a plan drawn up with the same logical forethought as distinguished his planning of engineering projects.
>
> "The evidence suggests that the main features of such plan (conscious or unconscious) were:
> 1. The ultimate objective to be the formation of a practice of his

own, and build this up steadily to a position in the forefront of British Consulting Engineers.
2. To achieve this objective, original solutions must be sought in all jobs better than orthodox and current practice would give – better in all respects (including economy) and so build up a reputation of 'good work – well done'.
3. Every avenue must be explored to obtain suitable work, and for this purpose to make the name of Oscar Faber known to the public, to prospective clients, and to architects as well as to fellow members of the engineering profession."

These ends were to be met by writing books and articles, by presenting papers to professional and other bodies on original research or with descriptions of his own interesting projects showing wherever possible original techniques, by lecturing to architectural and to engineering students, by serving on Institution committees leading eventually to election as President, and so on. Altogether he wrote eleven books, at least thirty papers to learned institutions, and many articles printed in the technical press. Not bad for a busy man whose real income came from practical engineering achievements in setting up and running his own firm. Along with all this he was spending time on his music and art with fair success, looking after his family life with rather less than adequate attention, and trying his hand at tennis, golf and sailing, into all of which he put plenty of energy, though not always with such shining results. His background and education never took him anywhere near sport in the sense of hunting, shooting and fishing; but he was confident his engineering prowess would give him all he wanted in life without the need for social conformity. He was later to be disappointed in this. It is a fact that for all his talent and enormous energy directed to fine ends, he was never knighted.

His first job on leaving college was as an assistant engineer working for the Associated Portland Cement Manufacturers Ltd. Here he had the good fortune of working closely under the Chief Engineer, Mr. Percy Taylor, himself a civil engineer of noteworthy standing and courage, always interested to apply his technical ability to unusual problems, leading, on a number of occasions, to novel solutions. And as with Professor Unwin at the Central Technical College, Taylor had a natural gift for disciplined accuracy in his use of the English language. There can be little doubt that at this stage in his life Faber was pursuing his enthusiasm for concrete work, with a particular bias towards its application to civil engineering. It was to be a curious succession of accidental events that slowly re-directed him rather towards buildings, and work with architects.

Much of the experience he gained with the APCM was to do with wharves and jetties: of particular impression was the construction in the Thames of the jetty to serve Swanscombe Works. This structure was constructed on timber piles, and comprised precast concrete piers 5ft 6ins diameter spaced 28ft apart, supporting a deck system of precast concrete beams. For the year 1906, precast work on this scale certainly demonstrated great courage and ingenuity by its designers. Faber had shared in the design-work, and later went out on site to act as Resident Engineer for the construction.

Also at the APCM, Faber became involved in the problem of constructing tall industrial chimneys at the Company's various works; and together a design theory was devised by Taylor, Glenday (his Assistant) and Faber and subsequently described and published in 1908 in the magazine *Engineering* under the title 'The Design of Ferroconcrete Chimneys'. The theory still stands good to this day. In the form it was expressed, the procedure of design necessitated some judgement and a laborious exercise of trial and error. Fifty years later, and after Faber's death, the firm he had founded sorted this out by preparing curves for direct design use; they also developed a much better understanding of the effects of temperature and oscillation. Nevertheless the original structural analysis of 1908 remains sound.

From the APCM, Faber moved to the large design-and-construct firm, Indented Bar Company (later to become Isteg, later again Tentor), where he worked under R. W. Vawdrey on the design of reinforced-concrete structures, most notably the factory for the The Gramophone Company (now EMI Records) at Hayes. It was working at Indented Bar he found himself with P. G. Bowie with whom he wrote the book *Reinforced Concrete Design: Vol 1 — Theory*. This was first published in 1912, and was the first great marker putting the name of Oscar Faber on the map. Whereas the early French engineers had for commercial reasons been shrouding the design of reinforced-concrete work in abstruse mystery, Faber and Bowie came out clearly and simply with a full *exposé* of how this composite material behaves under stress in elastic conditions, and how monolithic structures constructed in the material are to be analysed. It was an authoritative work, written in easy style, with all the wearisome supporting maths thrown into appendices at the end. It filled an immediate need, and was a best-seller at home and in other English-speaking countries. There were few engineering offices or colleges at that time that did not carry a copy of this book on their shelves.

With this achievement under his belt, Faber was able to get for himself at the relatively tender age of twenty-six the position of Chief Engineer at George Trollope & Sons and Colls & Sons Ltd. - later to become Trollope & Colls Ltd. - one of London's largest contractors of high repute in building and public works (now absorbed within the Trafalgar House empire). His first task there was to set up and organise a new department for the design and erection of structures in steelwork and reinforced concrete; and this department has continued through to the present day. His responsibilities included the construction of tall industrial chimneys, coal bunkers, water-towers and reservoirs, as well as many large buildings in London including Finsbury Circus House and the Hong Kong & Shanghai Bank, and in Shanghai the Chartered Bank of India, the Yokohama Specie Bank, and another building for the Hong Kong & Shanghai Bank.

All this work on buildings, particularly the detail-drawings needed for the work in Shanghai, brought Faber into closer touch with structural steelwork where he had a lot of fresh finding-out to do, which led him in 1914 to write his paper entitled 'Design of Steel and Reinforced Concrete Pillars.' This paper devoted fifteen pages to steelwork design, and the remaining three pages to saying that reinforced-concrete design was already perfectly well covered in the Faber and Bowie book!

In December 1913, Oscar Faber had married Helen Joan Mainwaring. This was a surprising match: he a boisterous restless selfish extrovert, she a gentle loving sensitive creature. That the marriage held together right through till the time of his death is a wonder: no one else could have handled him so well, or would have had the patience to do so. In about twenty years time the relationship was to start becoming tiresome.

Joan was a wonderful woman. She was the eldest child of Dr. John Gordon Mainwaring and Anna Hoefken. She had four strong-willed rebel brothers, who, as soon as their father died of cancer in 1906, went off to Canada taking their mother with them, and leaving Joan behind, alone, aged 26. Dr. Mainwaring was one of fourteen children of Dr. William Mainwaring, who was married in succession to sisters Mary and Ester, both daughters of Alexander Gordon, a Scot who had come down to Dudley near Birmingham to make his fortune out of wines and spirits. Alexander was a devout Wesleyan – indeed a personal friend of John Wesley – and son of a schoolmaster John Gordon, himself the son of a schoolmaster William Gordon. These Gordons were careful, thrifty people – as was Joan. Alexander Gordon, the wines and spirits merchant, was an acqaintance of Alexander Gordon of Gordon's Gin. So Oscar, four generations from Rasmus the Copenhagen brewer, had married Joan, three generations from Gordon's Gin. The marriage produced two daughters, Eileen and Barbara, and one son, myself, who would play a major part in the task of redeveloping the firm of Oscar Faber & Partners through the sixties.

Now the horror of the Great War descended upon everything. Trollope & Colls's activities switched from civilian work to

Government and Services projects connected with the war effort. Amongst the more interesting of the jobs Faber was to handle in this period was the design and construction of reinforced-concrete barges – steel being in short supply due to armaments needs. He also became involved in the development of non-magnetic naval mines for use in sealing off the low-country sea outlets from which the German submarines were operating. Faber designed the casings in concrete with non-ferrous alloy reinforcements, for which work he was awarded the OBE: Professor E. H. Lamb worked on the inner mechanisms. This was the same Professor Lamb under whom C. R. Glover (Bob) studied for his degree in civil engineering at the East London College (now Queen Mary College), and who subsequently recommended Glover to apply to Faber for a job in 1924 – which is how Bob Glover became what turned out to be a very important member of Oscar Faber's firm.

Meanwhile Faber had been continuing his full-scale tests on concrete beams at both the City & Guilds and the Northern Polytechnic Institute (now Polytechnic of North London). He had started these whilst with the Indented Bar Co. because of the general uncertainty of how concrete beams – weak in tension – could behave in shear, whether reinforced or not. This study continued over a period of about five years, in which time Faber solved the enigma of the inner mechanisms of stress behaviour within a concrete beam, and by what methods one could design the appropriate reinforcements to greatest advantage. It is interesting that in the Faber and Bowie book, Vol. 1, he could at that early time (1912) already have written:

> "If a beam or similar member is subjected to an external shearing force, internal stresses are produced, which are sometimes called shearing stresses; they are, however, generally very complex, and are to be distinguished from the shear stress produced in a punching machine, for instance. For this reason, the former stresses should be referred to as 'secondary stresses due to shear'."

This research work was to set the second great milestone in Faber's career. From it he prepared his splendid thesis entitled 'Researches on Reinforced Concrete Beams with New Formulae for Resistance to Shear', for which in 1915 he was awarded his Doctor of Science degree. For a man whose livelihood came from practical design and construction work (not a research boffin) this was a rare achievement at the modest age of twenty-nine.

Consistent with his determination for publicity he immediately had the thesis reproduced in serialised form in the magazine *Concrete and Constructural Engineering*. At the same time he gave the same material as a paper to the Concrete Institute. In both these he referred again to Vol. 1 of the Faber & Bowie book, and quickly proceeded to get Vol. II published (this time without Bowie) containing the fuller treatment of his latest work on shear. Later, in 1924, out came another book, *Reinforced Concrete Beams in Bending and Shear*, containing almost the same words and the same diagrams!

This latter book again shows Faber's extraordinary foresight. In the Introduction, in a period when all design work was being done on the elastic theory, he wrote what is so close to the modern limit state concept that it has to be quoted here at length to be fully appreciated. It is perhaps the best example on record of Faber's extreme far-sightedness.

"The method of experiment adopted in these researches is almost entirely that of constructing a series of test specimens in which all the factors determining their strength are, as far as possible, kept constant except the one factor immediately under consideration, and the specimens are then tested to destruction. The 'safe load' of the specimens is then calculated by the formulae which it is sought to test, and by comparing this with the experimental 'ultimate load' the factor of safety is determined. If this factor is found to be sensibly constant through a wide range of variation of the variable, and of the correct order, the formula is taken to be sensibly correct.

"It is only fair to state that a school of thought exists among engineers which would base all calculations on the elastic limit, and not on the ultimate strength. Members of this school point out that nearly all rational formulae (as opposed to empirical) – and all those considered in these researches are claimed as 'rational' – assume that plane sections remain plain after bending, and assume the proportionality between stress and strain. They argue

1. that as these assumptions cease to be correct at the elastic limit the formulae must not be used beyond it, and
2. that the examination of ultimate strengths gives no indication of the conditions prevailing at ordinary loads.
    Further they argue
3. that as the formulae which are justified by consideration of ultimate strength only cannot be considered by them as quite rational, but are to some extent empirical, they are only safe for structures exactly similar in dimensions, form, and other conditions to one already tested. The only method which they allow is the study within elastic limits and formulae based on such study.

"The writer appreciates the logic of these arguments. He feels, however, that though the study within elastic limits is free

from the above objections, it has objections of its own, some of which may be enumerated as follows:
1. Some materials, particularly brittle materials, such as concrete, have no well-defined elastic limits, and to work on 'a factor of safety of two on the elastic limit', which the school referred to prefers to a factor of four on the ultimate load, has very little meaning. This is particularly true in the case of reinforced concrete, where the concrete fails in tension when the steel is still well within its elastic limit, and in beams of such a composite material proportionality of load and deflection does not exist even within working loads, and a factor of safety based on its limit can therefore at best have only a very limited meaning.
2. Experimental difficulties of measuring stresses within elastic limits are always considerable; but in the case of reinforced concrete they are in many cases almost insuperable. With a long section of beam under constant moment it may be possible to measure the extension carefully, but even then the extension of the outside of the concrete near a steel rod is not necessarily that of the rod, which may have slipped to an unknown extent. If the steel is exposed for direct measurement of extension, the 'adhesion' and other essential factors may be seriously altered. When we come to such matters as shear stresses and adhesion stresses in complicated arrangements of reinforcement the method seems to fail completely.
3. For the above reasons the errors of experiment may lead to worse errors than the want of absolute rationality in the formulae.
4. Apart from the fact that the formulae become less rational when the elastic limit is passed, it is really the factor of safety on ultimate loads which is of most immediate practical value. An engineer is more concerned with what load his beam will carry than at what load the proportionality of load and deflection ceases. Indeed, even if there were no experimental difficulties in the elastic limit method it is doubtful whether it is always what is wanted. Suppose, for example, beam 'A' will carry two tons without exceeding the elastic limit of any of its constituent parts and will not fail before eight tons, and beam 'B' will carry two tons within elastic limits and will fail at three tons, most engineers would be willing to load 'A' up to twice 'B'.

"The writer, in his practice, endeavours to have regard to elastic limit *and* ultimate strength, and considers that an engineer who couples practical experience with theoretical and experimental knowledge and skill can generally determine which, in any particular case, is the determining factor."

These words from the Introduction to his 1924 book show that even then Faber was questioning the use of the *elastic theory* as applied to reinforced-concrete design, and how his mind was already moving towards the idea of *limit state design* nearly fifty years ahead of this concept being adopted by the British Code of Practice for Structural Concrete in 1972.

If there be any doubt at all that Faber had had a 'career-plan' from the start, there can certainly be no doubt he had developed a plan for his career by the time of his joining Trollope & Colls. When the Agreement for his employment was being prepared, he succeeded in persuading the directors that, subject to priority being given to T & C jobs, he might undertake on his own account whatever other appointments he chose, and subsequently, on giving suitable notice, give up his position as Chief Engineer to the Company, take his own clients away with him and so establish his own private practice, and in addition be retained by Trollope & Colls as their Consultant. Not a bad bargain for a man to strike at the age of twenty-six! And this is precisely how it worked out in 1921 when he launched out on his own, taking with him as much of the T & C staff as he needed for his immediate purposes. One of these was Jim Vaughan, then a young graduate.

The first recorded job in the firm, then known simply as the practice of Dr. Oscar Faber, was the Regent Cinema in Queen's Road, Brighton. The large glossy 20-page brochure, in colour, announcing the forthcoming opening, boasted this House of Entertainment would be the thirty-fourth Picture Theatre of Provincial Cinematograph Theatres Ltd., the largest firm of Cinematograph Exhibitors in the Kingdom. It went on in Gerard Hoffnung style:

> "There are no pillars to obstruct the view. The balcony, constructed entirely of steel, is the largest theatre balcony in the Kingdom. It has a clear span of 110 feet and a projection of over 50 feet, a feat of no small engineering skill on the part of Dr. Oscar Faber, OBE, the consulting engineer."

So much for the extent of Faber's feets or feat!

Another early job in the Faber practice was the deep-water jetty for the APCM at their Bevan's Works about two miles downstream from the Swanscombe jetty referred to previously. Percy Taylor and Oscar Faber had kept in touch since those earlier days, and now they were to collaborate again, though this time with the roles reversed. Whereas the Swanscombe jetty had been constructed on massive concrete cylinders, Faber now designed a structure of remarkable anatomy for the jetty at Bevan's Works comprising raking piles in the form of large A-frames. Subsequently Taylor and Faber described this work in a Paper to the Institution of Civil Engineers. The President of the Institution, in moving the vote of thanks, was reported as saying:

> "The Paper must be very interesting to those who had been concerned in the construction and maintenance of marine works of the character described by the Authors. Formerly works of that kind had been almost entirely of either cylinder or timber-pile construction, but the advent of the reinforced-concrete pile had provided another means of construction giving greater permanence than timber piling and probably greater economy than cylinder construction. The difficulty hitherto had been to secure adequate lateral strength to withstand the impact of shipping. That point had been dealt with very ingeniously by the authors' system of raking piles connected to the deck and by the provision of detached timber piling in front of the jetty, protected again by floating booms."

The ingenuity referred to by the President was typical of Faber's vigorous, questioning and fertile mind. Always he took an essentially simple and incisive approach to engineering problems – always prepared to reject such parts of orthodox solutions as he considered invalid or uneconomical – and search for something better by applying clear logical thought to the elements of the problem. Once he was sure in his own mind of the correctness of such a new solution, he would hold to it against all opposition, arguing his case with formidable skill.

Amongst his many gifts was his ability to express his thoughts in logical sequence and clear language, without being diverted to side issues. His tongue was a remarkably good servant of his brain. Indeed he might have made as good a barrister as an engineer. He was certainly an excellent expert witness in court cases. Many were the times in committee and other meetings that he would cut short a rambling aimless discussion with a few clear-cut words which dealt so completely with the point at issue that further discussion was seen to be unnecessary.

Following the triumph of his early researches and published books, one might have thought he would have enough to do in coping with his newly established practice. Not a bit! He now took upon himself the task of delivering regular courses of lectures on 'structures' and 'reinforced concrete' to post-graduate engineering students at the City and Guilds, and to architectural students at the Architectural Association in Bedford Square. Out of the material in these lectures came his two popular books *Reinforced Concrete*

Simply Explained (rewritten since his death) and *Constructional Steelwork Simply Explained*.

One of the gentler sides of his nature was his natural gift as a teacher. Apart from his great ability to express himself clearly and logically, he was able to appreciate the difficulty others might have in understanding things that were perfectly apparent to him; and with patience and kindness he could lower the plane of communication as necessary to achieve the best reception by his audience. This technique showed up well in his lectures and books. It was the same when working alongside him in matters of design and calculation, as also in discussion and argument getting to the root of a problem: he made it easy for others to follow and keep pace with his own rate of thinking.

Meanwhile he had been spending another two years on further research tests on concrete beams which led to his Paper in 1927 entitled 'Plastic Yield, Shrinkage, and Other Problems of Concrete, and their Effect on Design'. All these tests were carried out for him as a gesture of friendship by Mr. Harry Stanger. Most people consider that this was Faber's finest original research work and greatest contribution to the modern development and understanding of reinforced concrete. It certainly won him international fame. In later years the words 'plastic yield' came to be replaced by the word 'creep'.

It is interesting that after choosing in 1916 – very naturally – to deliver his paper on 'Shearing Resistance of Reinforced Concrete Beams' to the Concrete Institute, he subsequently changed course and delivered his subsequent papers on Bevan's Jetty and on Plastic Yield & Shrinkage to the Institution of Civil Engineers. There is no doubt his friends Mr. C. P. Taylor, Dr W. C. Unwin (Past President), Mr. R. H. H. Stanger and others had influenced him in this. The Concrete Institute had been sub-titling itself 'an institution for structural engineers, architects, etc.'; but when in 1923 it altered its name to the Institution of Structural Engineers, this was a specific narrowing of professional discipline not everyone might have wished for. Faber was interested in *concrete* right enough, but this didn't mean he wanted to limit his reputation to *structures*, which are only one part within the much broader range covered by the meaning of *civil engineering*.

However, following his Plastic Yield paper, Faber seems to have switched his course back again, realising that the Presidency of the Structurals would be the easier to attain (though it is known his desire was ultimately to reach that highest office at the Civils). Accordingly he proceeded to deliver one Paper each year to the Structurals (seemingly ignoring the Civils) until he became President of the Structurals in 1935. Then he devoted the first third of his Presidential Address to expressing a regret at the proliferation of splinter-Institutions, arguing the case for supporting the Civils as "the one great engineering Institution", and later "our Parent Institution". However by then he had rather branded himself as a structural engineer.

From that time he devoted his attentions back to the Civils, where he delivered six Papers in eight years (now seemingly ignoring the Structurals!). But already he had rather closed the Civils' door in his own face: never at the Civils was he even to become a Member of Council. It was a great pity, because he had in him all the right engineering qualities; but alas his bull-at-the-gate approach over some matters had been costing him a number of friendships and causing the build-up of certain pockets of resentment, as will be seen later.

Meanwhile an unfortunate event occurred in the mid-twenties in the course of constructing the foundations for one of the large banks in the City. A heavy party-wall about eighty feet high was in process of being underpinned as a 'series' operation. Too many of the 'series' had been taken out at one particular time, overstressing the clay beneath to such an extent that uncontrollable movement was set off. Jim Vaughan always remembered the telephone message to this effect coming through to Faber who, that Sunday morning, was on the court at the Coulsdon Tennis Club. Faber immediately went to his car, drove straight to London, and stood by, watching the party-wall slowly crumble and finally collapse. The whole event was a frightful anguish for him. There was nothing he could do but order that no human risks be taken. He remained, in the street, in his white flannels and black slippers – at one time eating a banana – until the worst had happened. His whole demeanour over this shocking disaster showed his tremendous guts. No doubt there had been a number of factors leading to the disaster; but it was typical of Faber that he stood forward staunchly, seeking in no way to shelter from any criticisms that might be made against his own firm.

Probably the greatest single achievement in Faber's working life, and certainly the one on which the reputation and continuity of his practice became soundly based, was his work on the design of the new Bank of England. This job came to him in his third year as a 'sole practitioner', and continued from 1924 till 1942, going through the periods of the General Strike of 1926, the Slump of 1931–32, and the start of the Second World War. He was to collaborate with an architect he had first come into contact with when working for Trollope & Colls – a Mr. Baker, later to become Sir Herbert Baker; and the relationship which sprang up between these two great men was to last their lifetimes. In the first instance Faber's appointment was as Civil and Structural Engineer; but after a period of time

Baker, finding the professional advice he was supposed to be getting from another engineer on the 'services side' was not forthcoming, enquired of Faber whether he could take on the Mechanical and Electrical Engineering work too. Faber immediately replied he could. In a personal letter to me, Rob Kell wrote:

> "Having taken a degree in electrical engineering, and having some general ideas on heating, he took on this added responsibility – without, in effect, having had any experience of such matters, or staff to do the design or supervision. It was only a man like him would address himself to such an undertaking.
> "I was a young pupil apprentice at the time with a Mr. Craig who was London Manager for a firm of heating contractors originating from Preston. Craig had done some jobs for Faber – Walpamur (the paint people), and the White Rock Music Pavilion at Hastings: and Oscar asked Craig if he knew of a person to join him for the Bank of England job – and Craig thought I would be the right chap. And so it happened."

Thus, Rob Kell, at the age of twenty-three, was landed with the M & E work of the Bank of England, working directly under Faber – and this was how Faber's firm became multi-disciplinary.

To emphasise Faber's self-confidence and courage in the whole of the Bank venture, one might look first at the foundation problem that had to be faced and resolved. It was a frightful responsibility, partly because of the scale of the work – even by today's standards – but more because of the relative dearth of soils knowledge and foundation techniques available at that time. The Bank covers a site of more than 4 acres, and the whole of this had to be excavated to a depth averaging about 45 feet for the construction of a basement floor, with two sub-levels of vaults beneath, and foundation works below that. There are more cubic feet of building at the Bank below ground than above. The task included underpinning the monumental Soane window-less boundary wall 200 years old, which it had been decided to retain, and at the same time providing a retaining-wall to support the pressures from the streets which come right up against the side of the building. These streets contain underground railways in Prince's Street and Threadneedle Street, as well as main sewers, water mains, hydraulic mains and electric cables. The slightest movement of the deep excavation face in the ground under the streets would have caused serious damage to each of these services. Meanwhile the integrity of Soane's wall had to be preserved as though sacrosanct. Faber devised and organised a scheme to avert these dangers by the use of precast concrete walings placed against the street face of each underpinning excavation, and jacking these off the frames of the timbering at the opposite face of the excavation, the jacking forces being calculated to balance the pressures from the ground depending on the depth below street level. This original technique proved to be entirely successful, and has of course since been copied by others in similar situations.

But the Bank of England job was just as outstanding in the conception of its mechanical and electrical works, and the integration of these services with the structural and civil works. In order to meet the possibility of siege conditions at the Bank – thinking back to the days of the Gordon Riots – Faber had the idea of providing a private generating-station within the precincts capable of supplying power for all purposes (there were, for example, some fifty lifts); independent water-supply from wells sunk under the lowest basement construction; and air-conditioning (then quite novel) as an essential ingredient to the whole concept – so much of the building being below ground and behind the Soane wall.

His bold scheme for the air-conditioning distribution system was a tunnel 8ft square below the lowest vault, from which shafts rose up through the basement floors and to the superstructure: copper circular branch ducts, concreted in the 2ft thick strong-room floors conveyed the air to each and every vault; and on the upper floors run-out ducts served all the various offices. The separate exhaust system took the form of a tunnel, 8ft high and 3ft wide, constructed within the thickness of the retaining-wall, and completely encircling the Bank on all four sides – Threadneedle Street, Prince's Street, Lothbury and Bartholomew Lane – and this tunnel picked up branch ducts as before. With Faber designing the raft, retaining-walls, strong-room walls and floors, he was in a position to combine structure and services in this unique way. The same tunnels and shafts served splendidly as routes for all main piping, electric cables and so on. For the superstructure there were twelve pressure shafts and twelve exhaust shafts, each provided with access doors and ladders from top to bottom – a total climb of about 150ft.

In his book *Architecture and Personalities* (1944) Sir Herbert Baker wrote:

> "A man to whom my thanks are due is Oscar Faber, who has collaborated with Scott and myself in designing both the structural and mechanical engineering works for most of our large buildings. The two services are generally given by different experts; but we have found the control of the two by one mind not only a help to the architects but also a distinct gain to the efficiency of the building operations. A modern building is such a complex organism that the steel skeleton and the arteries, veins, nerves, and all other parts of the structural body must be created in unison in themselves and with the structure of which they form so vital a part. Faber has been very

successful in our common enterprises. His work at the Bank of England presented many and great difficulties, not least of which was the underpinning of the high building to a depth of 60ft down in the clay subsoil, supporting the heavy traffic on surrounding streets and the weight of the high neighbouring buildings. This was done without an accident or claim for damage. I have much sympathy with the engineer who works on such buildings; his share of the creation is apt to be thrown into the shade by the high lights cast upon the architect. But at the Bank Faber's great work was recognized when heavy bombs fell on and near the Bank and the strucature withstood their blows to a remarkable degree; and again when the deep underground vaults proved equal to the strain of accommodating comfortably and healthily a very large population of workers during the air raids."

The whole scheme for the Bank of England is probably the greatest engineering work in connection with a monumental building ever handled in Britain, and is certainly Oscar Faber's personal masterpiece. It pointed the way for the future in so many of its features. Some of the hefty contributions Vaughan and Kell made to its successful execution are described in the chapter which follows. From Faber's own point of view, its magnificence had the effect of establishing his reputation as a *building-engineer* rather than as a *civil engineer.*

In 1935, following the experience of services work he had gained on the Bank and other jobs, Faber suggested to Rob Kell they were now in a position to prepare a series of articles on this subject for the *Architects Journal.* Faber made no bones about it; he wanted to get closer to Kell's know-how; also he was sure that by the discipline of writing, vague ideas would have to be crystalised, and many gaps filled in. The collaboration between the two worked well; and Faber was fortunate in finding that Kell's easy clear style in writing so matched his own that editorial work in assembling their respective contributions was minimal. These articles ran for a year.

Subsequently the articles served as a skeleton around which the famous Faber & Kell book *Heating and Air-conditioning of Buildings* was to be written and published in 1936. This book was an immediate triumph, meeting a long-felt need. It was quickly accepted as a standard work on its subject, and has since been kept up-to-date with numerous fresh editions. It put the name of J. R. Kell squarely on the map, and established Faber's firm as a leader in the field of heating and air-conditioning work. From the point of view of the art of services engineering there can be no doubt the book has made a great contribution to logical understanding and design, as well as to broadening the net which lures the increased number of young engineers required in this building discipline.

EARLIER CAREER

From Faber's point of view it emphasised further his growing interest in *buildings* rather than *civil engineering*.

Another job that ran through the twenties and thirties – essentially a personal Faber effort – was the underpinning of Durham Castle. It typifies Faber's boundless imagination in solving a problem most engineers, if similarly faced, would have regarded as beyond any practical solution. His concept was daring in conception and scale, and requiring much courage in execution.

Durham Castle is built on a hill which rises very steeply to a height of about 115 feet from the River Wear which surrounds it closely on three-quarters of its circumference, to the West, the South and the East. The building of the Castle was ordered by William the Conquerer following the Norman invasion in 1066. The Keep occupies the east part of the hill; this is linked via the Chapel and Senate Room to the Norman Gallery and the Great Hall at the west part. These buildings, up to about 70ft high, are constructed on sandy clay which in places had been brought in and tipped to a depth of about 15ft behind the outer battlement retaining-walls, which latter are founded about 30ft below Courtyard level on broken freestone and in some cases comparatively loose earth. Rock is not reached until a depth of about 70ft below Courtyard. The great walls of the buildings, having no footings or foundations and coming close to the battlement walls, were continuously on the move; some, about 7ft or 10ft thick, had tilted about $2\frac{1}{2}$ft by the year 1760. The $2\frac{1}{2}$ft overhangs had then been cut away and refaced; but by 1904 a further 9in. movement had taken place. In 1870 the lavatory block had parted company with the remainder, slithered down the hill and disappeared into the river; and it is no exaggeration to say the whole of the west fronts of the Norman Gallery and the Great Hall were on the point of following suit. Indeed the fact that the outer walls and the walls to the buildings were standing at all is made all the more remarkable when one realises that parts of the stonework was so loose it was literally dangerous to touch; and the effects of settlement had caused the stonework to bulge with cracks sometimes 2in. or 3in. wide.

The difficulties of the work were immense. The outer battlement walls, together with their underpinning, have to resist in addition to the downward weight, the outward pressure from the ground behind surcharged with the weight of the buildings upon it. The underpinning therefore had to be of greath width to meet this resultant inclined force – the widening coming outwards towards the face of the hill. To reach the rock at 70ft. depth, the operation involved excavating, within the precarious circumstances of the hill, a depth of 40ft below the battlement wall, to construct underpinning works to the profile of a gravity dam, varying in thickness from 13ft at their highest point, to 23ft at the bottom where they keyed into the rock. Had it been any ordinary structure, one would have started by putting raking shores to the walls and giving them lateral support, at the same time taking some of their weight on the shores. But in this situation the shores would have had to be at least 150ft long, and even then at a somewhat ineffectual angle and founded on most unsuitable ground. The only alternative was to tie the western front back into the hill; this was done using eleven pairs of $2\frac{1}{4}$in. diameter steel ties 120ft long (one tie in each pair situated 13ft below Courtyard level, the other about 31ft below) and securing these to reinforced concrete anchorages constructed in pits about 40ft deep, and 8ft by 4ft in plan, dug in the Courtyard. The ties of course had to pass under the buildings of the Norman Gallery and the Great Hall, necessitating 'prison-escape' tunnelling, gladly undertaken by local coal-miners otherwise out of work. But before it would be safe to do this, and before it would have been effective to have done it, the walls had to be strengthened so they would behave as homogeneous masses – and this was achieved by copious cement grouting under pressure. Altogether 42,500 gallons of cement grout was pumped into the walls; and this gives a good indication of the loose and rickety state they had been in.

Following the strengthening and tying and underpinning of the battlement walls, it became safe to underpin the walls of the buildings themselves. Owing to the tilt these had developed over the centuries, their centres of pressure were no longer central on their bases. The consequence was that pressures at the outside faces had grown to values in excess of three and four tons per square foot, and this on most indifferent ground: little wonder then, the increasing tendency for the walls to lean further! The principal object of the underpinning was to render the pressures uniform, so that any future settlements might be equal, with no further tendency for the walls to lean; accordingly it was designed so that the reinforced concrete foundations, instead of being central under the walls, were concentric about the lines of loading, and the bearing pressures on the ground uniform at something less than two tons per square foot. The space between the new concrete and the undersides of the old walls was then pinned up using blue brickwork. For the splendour of this whole operation, Durham University conferred upon Dr. Faber the Honorary Degree of Doctor of Civil Law.

In the earlier years of his practice, Faber took every opportunity he could of working abroad. After the 1914-18 War he had been appointed Consultant to the War Graves Commission and dealt with many of their foundation problems in Belguim and France, including for the Menin Gate at Ypres and the tall Canadian memorial at Vimy Ridge. Later he was appointed for the Customs House In Shanghai, for which the foundation problems again required his

EARLIER CAREER

personal study on site. Another early appointment was for the Bank of Athens, but though he paid a visit there, no more was seen of the job than just a roll of drawings and a modern Greek dictionary! A further overseas commission took him to India to act as assessor in a competition for a development scheme in the centre of Delhi. Here he found the bribery and corruption amongst the local officials intolerable: his recommendations were translated into the local tongue – but wisely, before signing this translated version, he took it to the British Embassy as a check, only to find the order in which he had placed the entries had been completely rearranged!

By 1935 Faber had reached the peak of his career. He was President of the Institution of Structural Engineers. He was supremely confident, boisterous, and covering an enormous amount of ground. He was still only forty-nine; his mind was clear and powerful; he was master of all around him. His Presidency was well deserved. Anyone who can remember the Structurals through the twenties and thirties will know that – along with their splendid Secretary, Major Reginald Maitland – no one made a more powerful contribution than Oscar Faber to building up that Institution to the reputation, strength and favour it was by then enjoying.

His Presidential Address was lucid, chatty, perhaps a little flowery. The last part was devoted to how, following completion of a project, credits are apportioned as between architects and engineers. In detail his approach was couched in terms of modesty and some delicacy of touch, but it is doubtful whether architects of the period would have been much enamoured of it. After warming to his point through careful and respectful preambles, he waded in:

> "One thing which has given thoughtful engineers some concern of recent years is a little carelessness in publications controlled by architectural bodies as to the credit for important engineering structures.
>
> "Thus in the RIBA catalogue of International Architecture, 1924–1934, we find Sydney Harbour Bridge and against it the name of a well-known firm of architects. No mention is made of the engineers who designed this bridge. The same thing happens in the Journal of the Architectural Association; for example, in April 1934, where again Ralph Freeman, who designed the Sydney Harbour Bridge, is not mentioned, but the name of a firm of architects is.
>
> "In the British Section of the Architecture display at the Brussels Exhibition was (and is) exhibited a photograph of the inside of the Mersey Tunnel with the name of an eminent architect under it and no mention of the engineers who designed and constructed the tunnel."

What good he expected would come from saying this before an

audience of engineers is not clear. It was a strange venue to be trying to handle such a sensitive matter. Surely he could not have imagined garbled versions would not get through to all architects. What he left unsaid in his Address was that at Sydney Harbour Bridge, Ralph Freeman (Senior) had consulted him professionally over the size and programming of the concrete pours for the massive foundations as a precaution against overheating on setting; and that at the Mersey Tunnel, Mott, Hay and Anderson had brought him in on the design of the reinforced concrete roadway! These 'assists' were close associations to really big civil engineering projects he would dearly have wished people to have known his firm had been involved in. Perhaps it was his supreme individualism that was the cause of all this message getting through only somewhat raggedly.

Notwithstanding this minor fracas, Oscar Faber's contributions to the art of structural engineering and to the Institution of Structural Engineers continue to be remembered with enormous respect. Indeed in 1966 – ten years after his death – a special annual award was established at the Institution, known as the Oscar Faber Award for the year's best paper published in the Journal and read at an Ordinary Meeting of the Institution, the award – at the discretion of the Council – taking the form of a silver or bronze medal or a diploma. The announcement of this award says:

> "Dr. Oscar Faber, Past President of the Institution (1935–36), will be remembered by generations of structural engineers for his work on concrete technology. ... The award will become a prized distinction among Chartered Engineers."

The sources of such accolade to the man seem almost endless, whether coming in his own time or years later – more such will be picked up in subsequent chapters. Meanwhile it is convenient now to turn the clock back to the early days of the firm Faber founded in 1921, and catch up on some of the other characters involved, seeing how they fit into the story and what sorts of tasks they were fulfilling through the twenties and thirties.

Harald Faber (1856–1944), Oscar Faber's father, when Danish Agricultural Commissioner in London.

Oscar Faber, in 1908, being prepared for diving to inspect the Swanscombe jetty on the Thames in Kent.

Steelwork for the balcony of the Regent Cinema in Brighton (early 1920s).

Underside of the cantilevered reinforced-concrete balcony slab for the grandstand at Lord's cricket ground (early 1920s).

Reinforced-concrete arched roof of the Royal Horticultural Hall, London.

Oscar Faber (1886–1956) at the time he was President of the Institution of Structural Engineers.

Joan Faber (1881–1967), Oscar Faber's wife, in the Hayes Court heyday of the 1930s.

Copper piping for panel-heating, ready for concreting to form the Soane domes at the Bank of England (1924-1942).

The generating station in the basement of The Bank of England – the waste products being conserved for heating within the building.

A. K. Lawrence's painting "The Builders" (1932) which hangs in The Bank of England. Sir Herbert Baker seated. Oscar Faber standing right foreground.

3

Jim Vaughan and Rob Kell

The two men who did more than any others to help build up the strength and great reputation of Oscar Faber's firm were Jim Vaughan and Rob Kell. Both greats in their own ways, it is difficult to imagine two men more dissimilar.

Vaughan was narrowly and superbly a structural engineer: Kell was broadly a mechanical engineer, but would happily let his mind wander to broader horizons. Vaughan graduated at University: Kell served as a pupil apprentice roughing it with boiler-makers and pipe-fitters. Vaughan had a purist streak about his engineering which sometimes sent him in long searches for unattainable perfection: Kell could see a practical way through most problems even ahead of the art of his discipline having envolved any proper theory. Vaughan could not delegate easily: Kell could and did. Thus Vaughan showed signs of overwork and worry: Kell did not – he somehow managed to switch off. Both were a delight to work with, being utterly loyal to the interests of the firm, and straightforward in all their dealings.

Vaughan was born in London in 1895, and educated at Skinners School, Tunbridge Wells, and Emanuel School, London. He entered the City & Guilds College at London University in 1912, but his course there was interrupted by the outbreak of the 1914–18 War. He joined the Buffs (now part of the 2nd Battalion The Queen's Regiment) and after a brief hotch-potch training on Salisbury Plain was pitched into battle in France in 1915. As a young raw lieutenant he was shot in the lower stomach when his battalion were mown down rushing the enemy line at Loos, and had to lie doggo the whole of that hot September day to avoid inviting further attention from the Germans whether by bullet or bayonet. The following night he was picked up as a prisoner and taken, seated in a truck, to a

German field-hospital where the initial treatment he received was barbaric. Subsequently he spent four months in hospital in Germany, of which period he has always spoken well of the excellence and humanity of the German doctor who attended him. From hospital he was transferred to his first prison camp, and thereafter shifted around from camp to camp over a period of three and a half years, suffering jail fever and picking up infections in his stomach and ears which were to plague him the rest of his life. The last six months of his prisoner days were spent on parole in Holland. There can be no doubt these horrible experiences were behind Vaughan's special satisfaction in his work involved with Faber in the construction of the Menin Gate War Memeorial at Ypres, fifteeen miles from the scene of the carnage he counted himself lucky to have survived.

Following his return to England and demobilisation, Vaughan went back, after nearly five years, to the City & Guilds and completed the final year of his civil engineering degree course in 1920. Jobs were scarce at that time; and virtually none was advertised. He called on a number of consulting engineers but without success. He then approached Faber, already well-known, and at that time Chief Engineer of Trollope & Colls. When they first met for interview Vaughan (twenty-five) was greatly surprised to find how young a man was Faber (thirty-four) and how impressive his overall bearing and stature. Out of this interview Vaughan was offered a job – "I want you to start tomorrow!" – subject to a month's probation period.

Faber's Engineering Department at T & C then totalled twenty-six, of which seven were working on outside sites. The next year, when Faber set up on his own at South Street, he took two of his T & C staff with him: one of these was Stanley Vaughan B.Sc., then on a salary of £260 *a year*, whom Faber gave the status of his Chief Assistant. A part-time shorthand typist and an office junior (tea boy) made up the full team. Vaughan was never quite clear how Faber had picked him, but believed it might have been because he had recently noticed on one of Vaughan's drawings of a reinforced concrete beam, the diagonal shear bars close to the support bent up more steeply than those nearer midspan. Faber had quizzed Vaughan on this, and seemed pleased with the answer he had got.

Despite the modest scale of the staff and the inauspicious style of the accommodation with its trestle-table furniture, the early days were tough, trying to keep the business afloat. Faber would never hear of having an overdraft facility: indeed his idea of respectable business was to keep as much money as possible lying idle at the bank – a philosophy he clung to, sometimes to quite bewildering proportions, right through to the end of his life. With his great reputation, all this discomfort was quite unnecessary; but he preferred to exercise his mind on matters of engineering which he understood, rather than worry about problems of accountancy with which he never felt quite at ease. But after all, it was his show, and his risk, so there was no reason why he should do things other than the way he preferred.

Right from these earliest days Vaughan found himself working closely at Faber's elbow for large parts of every day, sharing immediate problems and carrying forward Faber's instructions. Whether the problems were technical or otherwise, Faber valued going over them with Vaughan, and in this way a great mutual respect developed between the two. And so it was that Faber took Vaughan increasingly into his confidence, and for the next twenty years or so tended to turn to him for comment on most of the more difficult decisions in the firm. The choice was not surprising: Vaughan was the only person whose age reasonably matched Faber's – the others of the staff were generally some ten years younger, or more. Vaughan was looked up to by everyone as much the senior member of staff.

The amount of work in the office increased, but Vaughan noticed the care with which Faber deliberately held back the rate of growth of staff numbers! However after about six months, the first floor of the South Street house had to be taken to accommodate newcomers – these included Rob Kell, K. Montgomery-Smith (Monty), and Bob Glover. In spite of the cramped and inconvenient quarters, a considerable volume of work was now being carried through, largely the result of Faber's personal enthusiasm.

Vaughan found Faber a man of immense energy – particularly in these younger days – and quite tireless; and Faber expected his staff to match him in this. There would be frequent periods when 6 p.m. just came and went unnoticed, and all the staff were expected to stay on several hours to try and honour the optimistic promises Faber was apt to make. Vaughan lived only a couple of miles or so from Faber's home (whether Coulsdon or Kenley), and often when there was a difficult problem or a particular urgency, and the pressure and interruptions of the day prevented proper concentration in the office, the two of them would get together working in one or other of their homes, quite long sessions extending late into the night. Vaughan remembered well one occasion falling asleep over the dining-room table at 3 a.m., much to Faber's disgust: Faber appeared good for hours more, and next day turned up at the office at nine, bright eyed and bushy tailed, keen to get on again. The stimulation of all this made a great impression on Vaughan who regarded their close association as a great privilege.

Being so close to Faber in those early days meant that Vaughan was having a hand in practically every job going through the office. Whereas at Trollope & Colls he had been a new fish in a relatively large pool and under fairly close surveillance, he now found Faber happily giving him whatever scope Vaughan felt himself capable of handling. The two of them were having tremendous excitement and fun at this stage. Vaughan's widow, Maisie, five years Vaughan's junior, remembered well in her eighty-fourth year the thrill it had been in 1922 for her Jimmy, then aged twenty-seven, to be left to handle the Brighton Regent Cinema job, almost on his own. At the same time Vaughan was carrying the responsibility for the White Rock Music Pavilion at Hastings. Other work at Hastings, as well as many fine town halls about Southern England were to follow, all as a result of Vaughan's patient cooperation with the fine and sensitive architect for the Pavilion job – Cowles Voysey. Meanwhile much of Faber's effort at this time was being absorbed in other ways, such as research, lecturing and writing: he was also carrying the burden of negotiating fresh appointments, and handling the administration problems of staff, fee collection and other business matters. Hence Faber's appreciation and delight in realising Vaughan's great engineering competence.

Another early job (1923) Vaughan handled from South Street was the two-tier grandstand at Lord's Cricket Ground stretching the whole of one side of the ground in front of the main score-box (with its Father Time weather vane) and round and right across the Nursery End of the ground. This reinforced-concrete structure, far in advance of its time, comprises a sloping suspended deck measuring 48 feet from front to rear, supported by opposed cantilevers balanced about a system of central columns spaced 19 feet apart along the length of the stand. By means of this design, spectators on the lower covered lever have an unimpeded view of the play. The architect was Herbert Baker. The stands continue in successful use after sixty-five years. Later, in 1930, Vaughan was to design the steel roof over the Mound Stand, which carried on from the Nursery End along the other side of the ground paralled to St. John's Wood Road as far as the smaller score-box.

A fascinating job (1924) requiring a bold design that kept Faber and Vaughan up many nights was the Custom-House in Shanghai. This building had to be founded on soft mud, several hundreds of feet deep, being the fine material brought down by the River Yangtse. This mud becomes progressively softer as greater depths are reached, the top having to some extent been sun-dried to form something approaching a relative crust. The Custom-House is 450ft long by 140ft wide, comprising nine storeys and a tower 265 ft high at the front end, but only seven storeys at the back. The tower end comes right on the river embankment (the Bund) and still overlooks all the other important buildings in the area. It was clear that the load of such a building could not be carried on the embankment alone; nor could it be carried by piles alone, since the piles merely transfer the load to the softer mud below, where they are subject to settlement, which immediately brings the carrying capacity of the ground under the raft foundation back into play whether one likes it or not. The raft itself is of course also subject to settlement due to gradual squeezing out of pore-water – yet the raft-settlement characteristics would not be likely to coincide with the characteristics of settlement of any loads one might assess the piles as likely to be carrying. If a safe pressure under the raft were to be assumed as $\frac{3}{4}$ tons per square foot, about two-thirds the load from the tower would have to be carried on piles; yet at the back of the building only about one-third of the load would come onto the piles. There was a limit to the number of piles under the tower the soft mud could safely support; and there was no solution in providing a disproportionate number of piles under the remainder of the building, because this would only have the effect of reducing the settlement at the back, causing the tower at the front to tilt forward towards the river. A final settlement of 12 inches was anticipated and allowed for by building the ground floor up by this amount and providing two steps at the entrances to be moved as settlement proceeded. In spite of the fact that the front of the raft was carried on piles 4 feet apart, centre to centre in both directions, and the back of the building was relatively sparsely piled, the settlements turned out to be extremely uniform with no damage to superstructure, and very much of the order expected.

When Faber was appointed in 1924 for the Bank of England, Vaughan was of course most closely associated with all the detail work of the steel frame and its foundation. The latter consists of a reinforced concrete raft 4 feet thick which carries, without additional reinforcement, column loads up to about 350 tons. Where column loads exceed this figure (and in some cases they are over 1000 tons) additional reinforcement in the raft was provided locally in the form of large mats of steel rods, which under the most heavily loaded columns comprised approximately forty $1\frac{1}{4}$-inch rods in two directions at right angles, i.e. approximately eighty rods in all. This avoided the need for grillage joists at the feet of the columns – in those days normal for spreading such heavy loads onto the ground. Instead, the columns were seated merely on steel bloom bases which, in the case of the largest columns, are 6ft square and 9in. thick in a single slab of steel weighing approximately 6 tons. In this way a great saving of steel was achieved as compared with the large and heavy gusset-plates which would have been required with the old-fashioned type of base then in common use; furthermore the need was avoided to take the raft down such further depth (6 or 8ft) as would accommodate the gusset-plates below the level of the sub-vault floor. These effects, taken together, made for a considerable saving in the overall cost of the building.

But before saying any more about the detail work at the Bank, we need to look back to the early training of Rob Kell who was to have so much to do with the coordination of the M & E services. Kell came into engineering the hard way. He left school just after the end of the 1914-18 War, having taken the Cambridge Higher Examination - roughly equivalent to the present 'A' levels. He had no opportunity of getting a place at a university; many such places were in any case being taken up by the flood of men being demobilised from the forces returning to complete their studies. There was no National College in those days, and Kell had to pick up his training and experience as best he could as a pupil apprentice with a firm engaged in the manufacture of castings and boilers, and spigot and socket piping.

This practical background of seeing sectional boilers pulled together, and pipes laid and jointed, and knowing how the systems worked as a whole - often gravity systems then - formed the basis of Kell's extraordinary horse-sense in handling all matters of mechanical engineering. With all the theory he picked up in later life, and all the research and development studies he became concerned with, Kell always kept his eye on the main ball of ensuring the system he had designed *really could be made to work*. The genuineness of this was apparent whenever he visited the jobs as they approached completion: a smile of modest pleasure would spread across his face as he saw what had been created was actually functioning, had met the needs of the performance specification, and was responding properly to its controls.

Kell was only twenty-three when Oscar Faber took him on. Faber himself was only thirty-nine, with no design or practical experience of services work. One could hardly envisage a less probable team for tackling a job the size and complexity of the Bank. Faber was still operating from his South Street office. Baker had not yet prepared his plans in any sort of detail, so there was no services' work ready to get on with, and Kell was put on to tracing on linen a drawing of a concrete pile for the APCM Bevan's jetty! It was a curious beginning, but Kell was well fitted to take it all philosophically. After all, he had faced rougher surprises in his apprenticeship in the shops working alongside boiler makers with their varying standards of language, behaviour, and other qualities.

The work on the Bank was to prove very different from anything Kell had done before: he had to extend his mind now to generating-plant, lifts, well-boring, and pumping. Faber had already obtained the Bank's approval to appoint Rosser & Russell as heating contractors, and Drake & Gorham as electrical contractors, and these excellent firms produced the whole of the necessary detailed M & E drawings to Faber's overall conception. Kell's job was to co-ordinate all this; and much of his time was spent on the builders-work drawings for the tunnels and shafts which had to be integrated and sensitive to the intentions and needs of the architect. By this process Kell was able to watch and learn, indeed scrutinise, a tremendous range of work from a fine vantage point. It was a heaven-sent opportunity, and he enjoyed and benefitted from every moment of it.

His difficulty was how to sit-in at discussions on such topics and make intelligent comment without running the risk of exposing areas of total ignorance. No doubt this experience helped him consolidate his habit of checking all ideas back to first principles and adding a good measure of common sense. These were the circumstances that brought him quickly so close to Faber – Faber being in much the same boat himself! Both would keep an open mind on any subject, never rejecting out-of-hand any promising new idea. Neither was bound by any rigid rules or restrictions; indeed, at that time, neither had any!

What Kell liked was the way Faber could study a complicated problem, and in due course boil this down to its essential core. All side issues would be pushed out of the way, leaving only the nub to be attacked. Faber would then propound his own soloution – often delightfully simple – sometimes a little over-simple; and with Kell's comment and suggestions, Faber would do a re-think and follow the idea through with his own reasoning. It was this sort of joint effort, one man sparking off another, and eventually hammering out a solution, that became a working characteristic of Faber's firm.

From 1925 onwards was the period when panel heating was becoming popular. Crittall's held the proprietary rights for the panel-heating system which they let out to half a dozen licencees of which Rosser & Russell were one. Kell had never had anything to do with panel heating, so Faber sent him round to see some of the jobs being done at the time, which amongst others included Austin Reed in Regent Street, and University College Hospital Medical School. Although steel pipe had been used initially for such systems, these two jobs and others were now using lead-compo pipe – this being regarded as the very latest thing. The pipe was not embedded in the concrete slabs, but clipped up to the soffite and plastered over. Kell was horrified at all this, knowing that lead pipe expands with heat but does not contract. Faber was equally against the lead, and also against steel pipe for the Bank of England, since this building was expected to last for some hundreds of years. His idea was to use copper which was just becoming available in 150 foot rolls, half hard, or semi-annealed. Copper pipes have the advantages of being easier to bend than steel pipes and are free from risk of external corrosion; they also give a smoother bore, whereby the resistance of the water in long lengths of pipe is reduced. Furthermore, with such long lengths being available, a panel pipe can be taken from a riser and back to the return pipe without the need for any joints between these two points, which themselves can be made easily accessible.

Faber's firm was the first to use copper pipe for this purpose in the County Fire Office in Piccadilly Circus in 1925. The pipe was about 5/8th inch bore, laid and spaced on the timber formwork at 6-inch centres and concreted in. Following this experience the method was used throughout the Bank of England including the Soane domes which are a feature of the ground-floor banking halls. Here Faber introduced another innovation in the matter of the key for the plaster, avoiding hacking of the hardened concrete surface; instead, he had laid on the formwork a thin mat of rubber containing on its upper surface ribs ¼-inch square at ½-inch centres. After the concrete had been cast and the formwork removed, the rubber sheeting could be pulled away for re-use, leaving an effective grooved surface to receive the plaster.

It was in the planning and design of the generating station in the Bank of England that Kell's job really got off the ground. This involved problems and decisions that could not properly have been left for the heating contractors to settle. With the low temperature of the circulating water for the panel heating system (about 110°F), it was found possible to utilise this water for the cooling of the diesel engines. (This would not have been possible with a normal 'radiator' system running at about 180°F.) Using the heat from the cylinder jackets in this way increased the economy of the generating station by about 30 per cent. A further economy was achieved by delivering the exhaust gases from the engines into waste-heat boilers, so converting a further 15 per cent of the heat value of the fuel into useful heat serving other needs of the building. Thus the efficiency of the generating station in its use of diesel fuel was increased from the normal 30 per cent from just producing electricity, to 30 per cent (to electricity) plus another 30 per cent (from cylinder jackets) plus 15 per cent (from waste-heat boilers) giving a total thermal efficiency of 75 per cent. The waste-heat boilers were backed up by oil-fired main boilers. The whole of this plant was laid out spaciously in one fine engine-room occupying the double-storey height of the two levels of vaults on the Lothbury side of the Bank building. It must have taken Faber's mind back to the day he had organised a party of students to visit the power-station at Lots Road when he was at College in 1906.

Kell had many practical details to sort out over this whole installation, including the special design of the diesel engine jackets to withstand the great water-pressure from the 150ft height of the building; what to do with the waste-heat in the summertime; how to store enough oil to last six months or more. There was also the problem of the chimney which had the dual function of housing the exhaust pipes up to the roof. Of course the principle of using waste heat was not new, but the idea of using the cooling water from diesel engines for circulating in the panel-heating system of such a large, complicated, prestigious building was certainly enterprising and daring. Sixty years later the topic of saving energy is being heard everywhere as though it were something fresh; yet Faber and Kell had sorted it out and made it work successfully all this time before.

It was also at the Bank of England that Kell had his first involvement in the design of an extensive air-conditioning system. These were early days, and much of the plant available today had not been heard of. The scheme was to provide refrigeration plant to cool the main air supply – and have local re-warming coils to give some sort of control. In those days the only refrigerants in use on any scale were ammonia and CO_2. Ammonia had to be ruled out on safety grounds should there be a leak in the engine-room, and so CO_2 was adopted. This plant, mostly used for refrigerating ships, uses very heavy pressures with cumbersome coils and the like; nevertheless it all went in at the Bank and worked well. It was a pity Freon did not appear on the scene until many years later.

The water supply at the Bank started by the boring of two wells, and equipping them with deep-well pumps. These fed large water-storage tanks constructed below the sub-vault, from which the water was pumped to tanks in the roof for feeding the down services and the hot water calorifiers. Subsequently, as further phases of the Bank rebuilding came in, and also partly because the artesian basin below the City became over-pumped, more wells had to be bored, ending up eventually with nine in all. The experience of all this was carefully packed into Kell's memory-locker along with everything else.

It was in 1925 the firm made its move from South Street to much more commodious and agreeable premises at 37 Duke Street – between Oxford Street and Manchester Square, opposite the back corner of Selfridges. Here Faber and Vaughan were wrapped up together in the design of the reinforced-concrete structure for the Royal Horticultural Hall, off Vincent Square, Westminister (architects Easton & Robertson). The main hall comprises a central bay 72ft wide and 150ft long, on either side of which is an aisle 27ft wide. The central bay is spanned at regualar intervals of 21ft by concrete arch ribs 58ft clear height above ground floor, which carry a series of clerestory windows and roof flats forming a progression of steps. The two side aisles are roofed with a horizontal concrete slab 24ft above ground floor, pierced by 12ft diameter light openings.

Had the arches been parabolic from ground floor upwards, the thrust of the arch could of course have been taken care of quite simply at ground-floor level. But the architects required the arches, below the level of the aisle roofs, to stand vertically as normal building columns; and if then the arch had had to rely for its stability on a thrust at ground level, the eccentricity – and hence the bending moment – at aisle-roof level would have been so great that, apart from cost, the members could not have been made strong enough in anything like the size the architect wanted. The difficulty was overcome by treating the aisle roof slabs as horizontal girders of 150ft span and 27 depth, both girders taking a horizontal thrust of 45 tons from each arch rib – i.e. a total load of 270 tons per girder from the six arches – and tying these two opposing girders together at the ends of the hall with steel ties (135 tons) built within the end walls.

When, four years later, Vaughan had to design a similar arch construction for the Municipal Market Building in Nairobi – just slightly larger, 84ft wide and 62ft clear height – he persuaded the architects Rand Overy & Blackburne to adopt a form of arch more closely approaching a parabola, so that no horizontal girders or ties were necessary. The Nairobi arches are founded on rock quite close to ground level. Provision is made at the rear end for future extension of the hall, which of course could not have been achieved had there been a horizontal tie going across at an intermediate height.

Following the success of the stands at Lord's, Faber was appointed in 1927 for the stands at Northolt Park Racecourse. This was the time of the craze for pony-trotting (sulky racing). There were five stands in all, three known as 'Public' and fenced off separately from the Members Stand and the Grand Stand. The latter was a rather swish affair, 180ft by 90ft, with Royal Box, extensive restaurant facilities, and an upper Promenade with views out over the surrounding countryside. Its most striking engineering feature was its bold cantilever roof reaching forward 65ft over the whole of the stepped seating giving clear uninterrupted views forward and to both sides, the whole swept to a fine parabolic profile. The concept for this scheme was Faber; the detail was Vaughan. It was a delightful joint achievement. The contractors for the work were Holland, Hannan & Cubitts – and it was the firm's first contact with a young man Mr. F. S. Snow – later to become Sir Frederick Snow. Sadly the craze of pony-trotting was soon to fade; and other commerical pressures caused the stands to be demolished. Lucky for the demolition contractor they had been designed and built in steelwork and not in Faber's indestructible quality of reinforced concrete!

Mention has been made earlier of the deep-water jetty Faber

designed for the APCM at Bevan's Works on the Thames. Vaughan's initials appear on many of the calculations and drawings for this job too. A crisp comment on Faber's conception for the basic anatomy for this jetty is expressed in a letter Vaughan wrote fifty years afterwards:

> "What impressed me most at the time was the fact that the final detailed design approximated so closely to a 'thumb sketch' which Dr. Faber made as soon as he had digested the requirements."

Up to this sort of stage there was little going on in the firm that Vaughan did not know all about. The staff had reached about fifteen; over the next decade, to the start of the Second World War, it was to treble. Other members of staff were now being left to take increased responsibility, and Vaughan had necessarily to detach himself from close job detail in order to oversee the greater range of work he was entrusted to cover. One has to be careful therefore not to attribute to Vaughan effort in the office which others were making, and the responsibility these others were beginning to carry in their own rights. The next chapter aims to cover some of these other jobs spread across the firm.

But with the onset of war, when people got split up and sent out onto vast projects about the country, definitions of personal job responsibility started becoming clearer once more. And after the War, when Vaughan took charge of the office at Gray's Inn, his jobs were to become separate and recognisable from the remainder of the firm's structural effort which was based then around Dr. Faber at St. Albans. Some of Vaughan's jobs in Nigeria were particularly outstanding and get picked up later in the book.

Kell of course had his own special jobs too, like heating the Cathedrals of Canterbury, St. Albans, Durham and St. Paul's. But Kell's position was different. In the first place there was a mystery about his M & E work Faber had a great respect for; and Faber knew how badly he needed Kell's specialist competence. To the rest of the firm, Kell's was an art quite different from anything a civil engineering graduate had studied; in any case, what structural engineer would wish to bother with all these pipes and with blowing air about? Let Kell do his thing; the rest of the firm would make the structures sound and strong, which, at the time, seemed to them so much more important. But Kell's position was different in a second way. Whereas the senior structural staff each had their own jobs to handle and worry about, Kell and his little team – then only three or four – were getting involved in everyone else's jobs right across the board – Vaughan's, Monty's, Glover's, Budgen's. Later – after the War – starting about 1950, Kell's section was to grow to be the largest in the firm, occupying the whole of the four-storey building at 29 Queen Anne Street in London's West End between Harley Street and Wimpole Street.

So how was it the outsider came through? One explanation could be that in fifty years the attitude towards human comfort and convenience changed quite beyond measure: e.g. standards of lighting; standards of heating and quality of air – and the sophisticated control of these; standards of public health, plumbing and drainage; standards of lifts – ganged and equipped with memories; standards of call-systems, telephones, alarms; standards of fire-prevention and fire-fighting; standards of hospital equipment and services. All thse have advanced beyond recognition – whereas the buildings in which they have to be installed have not changed in basic need to quite the same degree. But the real explanations of Kell's great success was his willingness to grasp by the throat the situation he recognised himself to be in – an engineering discipline where decisions were being taken too much by rule-of-thumb methods, somewhat airy-fairy, even the result of unscientific guesswork; and he, in his dogged rational way, would weigh up any problem and the evidence available, make fresh enquiries or tests as he judged might be necessary, and eventually stick it out until some solution could be found which came up to his own ideas of practical reality.

A good example of this was his approach, in the mid-thirties, to the task of ventilating the Earls Court Exhibition Centre. This building is interesting as containing approximately 50 million cubic feet covering 12 acres and divided into a number of large halls which can be merged or separated as required. When separated, corridors between the separate halls are provided by double roller-shutters. The architect was Howard Crane whose skilful planning solved all the problems arising from such a novel arrangement.

The main central hall (Hall B) was 250ft span, 400ft long and 115ft high, containing about 11 million cubic feet. It has a large swimming pool in the middle at ground floor level, but this can be closed over for other uses by a false floor operated hydraulically rising from the bottom of the pool. The hall is designed for dual purpose – (a) for seated audiences for such events as circuses, tournaments, and when the swimming pool is in use, and (b) for exhibitions. Under condition (a), additional seating is brought in and supported on steppings which form an extension of the fixed stepped-seating at second-floor gallery level, passing in front of the gallery floor at first-floor level, and so down to ground-floor level, in this way making one great arena capable of seating 23,000 occupants.

From a ventilation point of view the problem was to provide an adequate and stimulating distribution of air, and at the same time satisfy the requirements of the London County Council in terms of smoke extraction. Due to the great distances from the road and entrances to the centre of the main floor, the L.C.C. concern was to make adequate provision for the direction of air currents to be away from the entrances and towards the centre. Extraction of air and smoke from the top they considered essential, particularly when the building was being used for exhibitions of what might be highly inflammable material. Hence distribution of air by nozzles pointing in a downward direction at times of exhibitions was not permitted: yet no other method would have been practicable for ventilating the hall when used for seated audiences, owing to the great distance between the centre and the periphery where alone ducts and ventilation plant could be housed. Low velocity air movement for seated audiences tends to give a sense of stuffiness and stagnation due simply to absence of movement of air over the skin. Kell wanted the blow from his nozzles to set up a sufficient turbulence for the audience to feel some sensible air movement.

The solution was to provide on the roof, above second-floor level, eight plants equally spaced about the 1300ft perimeter of the hall, each plant capable of providing a powerful blast of air blown through six high-level nozzles in a direction parallel to the slope of the seating and some 10ft above it. Extraction was two-thirds by ducts under the second- and first-floor galleries at the sides of the hall; the remaining one-third through the lighting slots in the main false ceiling, and thence via the roof space back to the plant space. The whole of the extract air being drawn back from the sides and roof into the plant is available for recirculation at times of initial warm-up: however by control of louvre dampers in the fresh-air intake, any desired balance of recirculated and fresh-air can be obtained.

When the hall is used for exhibitions, the dampers to the high-level nozzles are shut off, and the air inlet into the hall is achieved entirely by reversing the direction of flow in the ducts under the galleries at the edges of the hall; at the same time the dampers controlling the extract from roof space are opened wide, so that the whole of the extraction is from the top, as required to meet the needs of the L.C.C.

The distance from the nozzles above second floor to the centre of the hall at ground-floor level is about 140ft; and, in order to give some air movement at the centre of the hall, this was the length of blow required. At the time, there was no reliable information available on lengths of blow, so Faber and Kell instigated tests with the collaboration of Messrs. Norris Warming Co. and Messrs. Keith Blackman. One of the difficulties of tests of this kind is that if they are to be full-scale, they need to be done in a building the size of Earls Court; but Earls Court had not yet been built, and there was no other building anywhere comparable. When such tests are scaled down and carried out in smaller buildings, the essential conditions wanting to be explored are lost. And if tests with a single full-size nozzle were to be carried out, for example, in a railway tunnel, air movement might well be perceived half a mile from the nozzle; yet, placed on its own in a large open chamber, the same blow from the same nozzle might not be noticeable only 100ft away. These were the practical difficulties Kell had to steer the tests through; nevertheless the tests revealed certain basic truths, and the conclusions drawn from them settled the design of the particular nozzles that were eventually adopted.

For various nozzle sizes, the actual lengths of blow were measured for different velocities at the nozzle mouth. As was to be expected, increasing the velocity was found to increase the length of blow, though beyond a certain point little advantage was obtained by increase of nozzle speed. Furthermore increasing the size of the nozzle – i.e. the volume of air for a given velocity – also increased the length of blow. Thus, in rough terms, a nozzle 1 sq. ft. discharging at 3000ft per min gave a length of blow of 120ft, but at 1500ft per min gave a blow of only 60ft; and a nozzle ¼ sq. ft. at 3000 per min could produce a blow of 60ft, whereas at 1500ft per min it could blow only 30ft. The tests ranged over many nozzle areas and different velocities.

Another main purpose of the tests was to discover at what nozzle velocity could trouble from noise be expected. It was found that up to 2000ft per min there was no problem: above this, noise increased until at 2500ft per min it had reached the maximum that could be contemplated in a public building. Accordingly a velocity of 2300ft per min was selected, giving a length of blow of about 130ft for a nozzle of 3 sq. ft. aperture.

Considering the action of the nozzle, it was apparent there was an expanding cone of moving air delivered by the nozzle, this reducing in speed at increased distances from the nozzle. The air moving at the surface of the cone induces secondary currents in the surrounding air, thus setting in motion a much increased air volume, and in the process dissipating the energy of the main stream. On the basis of this hypothesis, it was clear the furthest length of blow would be obtained using a circular nozzle (this having the least perimeter for a given area). And so the matter was resolved.

When the first of the eight plants was ready for running, a test was carried out using the full-size nozzle before manufacture of the remainder was completed. Smoke bombs were released in the fresh-air intake, and observations made of the current of air discharged from the outlets. Even though only one plant was running, the smoke was projected well down below the first-floor gallery level, and within a short time it circulated in secondary currents diffusing itself almost completely over the whole of the hall. And so the pudding was proved!

Before rounding off this chapter and leaving Jim Vaughan and Rob Kell in their rightful places as part of the general fabric of Faber's firm up to the times of their retirements in the sixties, one cannot help just mentioning the job they did together in the thirties (Vaughan still only forty, Kell thirty-three) on the site of the old Royal Army Clothing Depot in Grosvenor Road, half a mile upstream from the Tate Art Gallery. This enterprising and speculative development by Messrs. Richard Costain – who also acted as the main contractors for the work – was to become known as Dolphin Square. It was the largest block of flats in Europe, covering a site of seven-and-a-half acres, the nine-storey building occupying the four sides of a square enclosing gardens of about three acres. The frontage on the Thames Embankment is 500 feet. The complex contains 1220 separate and self-contained flats. It is provided with a large underground garage and a sports centre with swimming pool, squash courts and a most efficient restaurant. The architect was Gordon Jeeves.

Before the job started in January 1936, Costains had already signed tenancies starting November the same year. Design and construction had to move apace. Costains built at the rate of one floor every ten days – right across the board – including all trades. People had been saying reinforced-concrete for building-frames was slower than steel construction; this job showed they were wrong, and really put concrete on the map. The work was organised with four separate gangs, each in sight of one another, working in competition, subject to daily bonus rewards for each member of the winning gang. The November 16th date was achieved, subject to tarpaulins over the lift wells, and one or two other scrambled innovations. It was an attitude of working in those days quite different from anything to be seen today.

For Rob Kell, the year 1936 was also a highlight because of publication of the book *Heating and Air-conditioning of Buildings* which he co-authored with Oscar Faber. There is little doubt this triumph was the making of Kell and the foundation of the M & E section he was to create and manage in the firm for the next thirty years. Jim Vaughan could write excellently, too, but unfortunately always hid his talent by ghosting for Faber. The two books *Reinforced Concrete Simply Explained* (1922) and *Constructional Steelwork Simply Explained* (1927) were largely from Vaughan's pen. Both were the republication of series of articles in technical magazines, the Concrete book having appeared in *Concrete & Constructional Engineering*, and the Steelwork book in *The Builder;* and sometimes Vaughan had been working on the manuscripts and diagrams for these the same day as he had had to run them round direct to the printers. Previously the same material had formed the basis of lectures Faber had been giving to students at the Architectural Association School, where on occasions – and then at the shortest notice – Vaughan had had to stand in and improvise from Faber's all too sketchy notes. Whilst Vaughan could write well and did not mind speaking before an audience, there was something sensitive and shy about him that tended to keep him out of the limelight. It was a pity he never wrote a book or an article under his own name, and never presented a paper other than his rather formal Presidential Address to the Structurals in 1955.

Kell, on the other hand, had the complete taste and flair for public speaking – and always with a fine modest dignity. At the St. Albans Debating Society he had followed in his brother Percy's footsteps and become President, a position he held for three years. His favourite adage on this was 'Stand up, speak up and shut up'; and Kell could do all three in the fullest sense, and splendidly. In 1944 he presented a most challenging paper to the Institution of Heating and Ventilating Engineers (now the Chartered Institution of Building Services) entitled 'Heating, Past, Present & Future'. Helped along with touches of light humour, he began by covering in some detail the early development of heating methods over the previous two hundred years. This he followed by comment on current progress so brief as almost to be disdainful: particular scorn he heaped on the inefficiency of solid-fuel boilers, then on the pipe-systems therefrom, and onto the standards of insulation techniques, and

> "at the end we allow whatever heat is left to escape in small parcels, at a much lower energy level than initially, and after that we lose interest in it: it has gone to the wall or the winds, we never know quite where."

He followed this by glimpsing in the future some of the things he felt the heating industry should be alerting itself to, such as the ideal of 'cool air and radiant warmth', the exploitation of the heat-pump principle, a rationalised design for solid-fuel boilers, a fuller use of all that we cover by the word 'electronics', and eventually – perhaps rather a long shot, this – a deeper study of the picture which modern physics presents of heat, light, and magnetism, electricity, chemistry, gravitation, the spectrum, and the periodic table all interconnected by the same system.

> "It appears that we as heating engineers will soon have to get our basic theory into register with this new conception. ... What for instance lies in the unknown gap between the shortest electric or wireless waves and the longest heat waves? Is there here a means of transmitting heat without pipes or wires?"

This startling paper had a very warm reception.

Kell's Presidential Address to the I.H.V.E. in 1952 was equally stimulating. He effectively banged the drum for technical progress by calling for more and better papers, urging a review of the whole field of research, and pressing for more data on many subjects to be gathered and marshalled. And with the same sort of foresight as shown in the paper previously referred to, he said:

> "Whereas in the past we have concentrated on the design of heating and ventilating systems for buildings to meet certain specified conditions, I suggest that we must see to it that we take a vital interest in the thermal properties of the building as a whole. The building and its heating installation must be considered together; and as much – if not more – can be done in the construction of the building to economise heat, as in the design of the boiler plant or warming apparatus."

Later he touched once more on his vision of the exploitation of modern physics to meet everyday needs in normal circumstances. Here he was talking of atomic energy and its relation to heating and ventilation.

> "What the future holds in this direction we cannot say, but I only mention this matter so that members may be reminded of it and lose no opportunity to make it well known that our concern in heating embraces every form and source of heat and is not confined to any one particular medium."

In 1958 Kell presented his paper entitled 'A Survey of Methods of Pressurisation of Hot-Water Systems'. This was most timely, the development and use of H.P.H.W. systems having moved on apace in the previous few years. Kell had produced a very complete survey and review of current practices, and to it he had added – as always – his own suggestions for future development and simplification. A particularly interesting part of the paper was the collected notes on the experience of others; and this was further enhanced by the lively discussion the paper stimulated, over a dozen speakers contributing, and Kell – in happy form – giving every bit as good as he got.

Another paper of Kell's, entitled 'Services and Air-Conditioning for Tall Buildings', was presented to the Structurals in 1961. This again was topical, and in its time something of a revelation to the audience he was addressing. It still stands as a fine overall appreciation of a highly specialised subject.

Altogether Kell wrote about twelve papers to learned Institutions, as well as numerous articles for the technical press. In his time he also updated the Heating and Air-Conditioning book through five editions, including the change from Imperial units to S.I. His easy knack for public speaking made him a popular lecturer to a variety of groups and associations about the country. A further measure of his ability and reputation for general coverage of his subject was the choice made by *Encyclopaedia Britannica* that he should write the sizeable entry for the 1975 edition of that tome covering the world's history and experience in Heating, Ventilating and Air-conditioning. In 1966 he was awarded the CBE for his contribution to the advancement of engineering.

Rob Kell was to die in 1983, sixteen years after his retirement. It was a great personal blow; and his wife was kind enough to allow me the privilege of reading the lesson at his Memorial Service in the Cathedral and Abbey Church of Saint Alban.

4

The Heyday of Romney House

Not much in real life fits nicely into watertight compartments to suit authors trying to write a biography divided conveniently into separate chapters. There are too many factors ebbing and flowing, all with different cyclical periods, and each to some degree out of phase with the others. Relationships with people, and associations with other firms, come and go as needs and opportunities change; operations and businesses vary in style and location, even from country to country; world and national economics never stand still, whether the result of commerce, social conscience, war or fear of it. Nevertheless one very recognisable period in the development of Oscar Faber's firm, neatly defined, triumphant, came in the thirties.

Economically this was another worrying and restless decade both at home and overseas. 1929 had seen the return of a Labour government, and the Prime Minister Ramsay MacDonald was to remain in power until 1935. The cause of the great Slump in the early thirties lay outside Great Britain, and largely in the general reliance of so many other nations on American prosperity and loans: but about 1930 these dried up abruptly when the great mood of speculation in the United States collapsed. This had the effect that British customers about the world could no longer afford to buy British goods, and British industries saw their export markets disappear. The number of registered unemployed *men* reached 3 million by the end of 1932. Then, as from about 1933, there was a general recovery of world trade. This was much to Britain's advantage, though the number of unemployed remained high right up to the start of the Second World War in 1939.

It was at the tail end of the twenties that Faber's staff showed signs of outgrowing the Duke Street office; furthermore the scale and complexity of the jobs being undertaken made it desirable to get the Firm shifted into better and more modern premises where greater flexibility of operating could be achieved. Just at that time Holloway Bros., who were the main contractors for the Bank of England, saw the chance to embark on a speculative venture (Holloway Properties Ltd.) and build a new office block in Westminster in Marsham Street, just north of Horseferry Road, and only a stone's throw from the Horticultural Hall. Because of the Bank team, it was a natural choice that Oscar Faber should be the engineer for the new building, and Rosser & Russell and Drake & Gorham the services contractors. Due to the Slump, construction costs were low; and the cheaper the building, the cheaper would be the rent. The building was completed in 1931 and given the name Romney House out of deference to little Romney Street. Sir Herbert Baker moved into the seventh floor at the top; Faber took accommodation immediately below him on the sixth floor; Rosser & Russell had the next floor down, the fifth. Everything had worked out very conveniently.

This was the best accommodation Faber was ever to work in. His own corner room was appropriately fine and furnished in bold masculine style: one of the walls was adorned with large-scale models of the Lord's and Northolt grandstands. Immediately adjacent to Faber was a small room for Miss Jones, his competent and long-serving secretary. The reference OF/JJ on letters and documents was well known and respected both inside the office and out. That duo held together a quarter of a century.

Faber was now approaching his zenith. Although he would never admit it, he must have known, for the first time in his life, all real financial worries were behind him. At the age of forty-five he was physically as strong as an ox, technically as widely competent as any engineer practising in his field, and certainly enjoying a carefully nurtured reputation of a very high order. Success, and the struggle to achieve it, were in fine balance, so that confidence was in his every action, tempered still with that modicum of modesty that makes a genius readily bearable. Fiendishly handsome, and as charming as he would choose to be, there were few hurdles that could have troubled him. He now had a well-proven staff, capable of supporting him in all his activities, suitably accommodated in pleasant conditions, and of a size he personally could control to whatever degree of detail he desired in terms of engineering, organisation and cost. It was as though he were the director, producer and conductor of his own orchestra.

This fortunate situation was to last nine years until the War, when various of the seniors were to be sent out to handle sizeable jobs on their own, largely out of reach of Faber, and in any case too extensive in detail for him to hope to keep tabs on. For example

Vaughan was then to run the Royal Ordnance filling factory (ROF) job at Kirkby near Liverpool in Lancashire; Glover was at the Magnesium Electron factory at Padiham thirty miles further north; while Kell, involved as always on all the firms M & E work, spent half his time commuting by car between Kirkby and a second ROF job at Risley about twenty miles away near Warrington. Faber meanwhile was then to operate from St. Albans with a relatively small staff of whom the most senior was Monty. After the War things were never to settle down again with Faber having the same direct control as he was able to exert over the compact team he had gathered together at Romney House in the thirties.

Apart from Faber's own room, and Miss Jones's, the remainder of the Romney House office was left as one large open plan. Kell and his small team – by virtue of their M & E services involvement in and amongst most of the jobs the structural engineers were doing – was kept closest to Faber: besides there was the mystique about Kell's discipline which necessitated him being handy on call at all times. In 1928 Kell had acquired the Firm's first air-conditioning experience by demonstrating the practical necessity for such a system at Lloyds Bank Head Office, Cornhill, where Faber was doing the engineering in collaboration with architects Campbell Jones Sons & Smithers. The need arose in a special basement room with 150 occupants permanently engaged, where the lighting load (in those days tungsten) was 20kW. It is clear that in a basement room of this character, where a large quantity of heat is given out both by the occupants and by the electric lights, there would be an intolerable increase in air temperatures unless mechanical ventilation were provided. Kell had calculated – and subsequently verified by testing when the room was completed – that even with eight air-changes an hour, there would be a temperature rise of 13°F between inlet and extract; so that in summer time, when the outside air might be 80° or 90°, the inside temperature would be more than 90° or 100° which would of course be quite unacceptable as a working condition. Accordingly a refrigeration plant was set up to bring the air inlet temperature down to about 55° so that even in the very hottest weather the temperature in the room was prevented from rising above 68°F.

The remainder of the seniors at Romney House could be recognised by the positions they occupied on the floor, and by the number and types of assistants or juniors they had attached to them. Vaughan had the best corner and more space than anyone else to spread out his team. A major thread running through the Romney House period was the succession of prestige buildings for which the architect was Sir Herbert Baker along with his co-principal Alexander Scott; and these jobs all came under Vaughan's wing. There was the Bank of England job still running on; also

Martins Bank Head Office, Glyn Mills Bank Head Office, and at various times work at Barclays Bank Head Office. These buildings were all of very high monumental standard, having great architectural dignity, and designed with no doubt that they would outlast a number of generations. All were heated by the copper-piped panel heating method. Other buildings with Sir Herbert Baker were the 'Empire buildings', including the Royal Empire Society (now the Royal Commonwealth Society) in Northumberland Avenue, India House, South Africa House, and Rhodes House, Oxford: also at this time were Church House, Wesminster and the Ninth Church of Christian Scientists in Marsham Street, Westminster. All these were of a prestige standard, special of their era, unlikely ever to be produced again.

An unusual problem arose in 1931 in supporting the roof and ceiling for the new Dining Hall at Haileybury College. Baker designed this to take the form of a shallow dome on a central square, 64ft across, with four bays projecting from the square with barrel vaulted roofs; and he wanted to keep the curve of these roofs as flat as possible, with the consequence that the steel arches carrying these roofs on the lines of the four sides of the square strike the corner abutments at a point about one-third down, but the dimensions for the brick abutments was nothing like sufficient to receive this thrust and still remain stable. No tie at the level of the springing of these arches could be considered architecturally, and the solution adopted was to introduce vertical steel trusses within the brickwork cavities so as to receive the thrusts at springing level, and tie these across the building with upper ties hidden within the roof, and lower ties buried below the floor.

A further thread through this period was a succession of work on town halls, particularly with the architect Cowles Voysey. Voysey became highly specialised in town halls; he seemed always to have one on the stocks, and knew instinctively how to plan a council chamber, and how many committee rooms were needed. After Hastings, the firm enjoyed working with him on town halls at Bognor, Worthing, Bromley, Watford, Winchester and Hull – also on the Cambridge Guildhall. At this time the firm also engineered the Wembley Town Hall with architect Clifford Strange; and High Wycombe Town Hall with architect R. G. Brocklehurst – Cowles Voysey acting as consulting architect.

Other seniors at Romney House were Monty and Glover and W. E. J. Budgen (another Jim – though in those days first names were not used anywhere down the line; everything was surnames). Monty always had a lovable sense of artful fun about him, whether in the office or out. Whatever car he was driving at the time, you could be sure many of the maker's parts had been replaced or augmented by home-made devices of special cunning, whether of tin-can, string, wire, or rubber tubing. He came back from one holiday having repaired his radiator with a cement mortar. And it was Monty who, when Vaughan's wife was two week overdue with her first baby, drove down from London in his sturdy tourer and bounced her round the country lanes of Surrey. Whether it was the harsh springs of the car, or the ruts in the lanes, or Monty's driving, or all three, we shall never know; but within a few hours Maisie Vaughan was delivered of a fine son.

Monty had joined Faber at South Street in 1922. Always with an enthusiastic enquiring mind, he liked to follow closely Faber's various research exercises, and gave a good deal of his own time to help by taking actual measurements and readings of physical tests and experiments. Whereas through the twenties Vaughan's name would figure in the 'acknowledgements' at the ends of Faber's published papers, as from the thirties this tended to become more often Monty's. In the open plan of Romney House Monty took up a central and strategic position, equidistant from Kell and Vaughan, and with a clear sight of the door to Faber's room. Not much of any interest escaped his notice from there.

It would be wrong to say anyone in the firm had a narrow speciality within their own discipline. Things worked out in a much more general fashion than this, each member of staff tending to turn his hand to whatever job should come along, provided of course his team at the time had the capacity to cope. Nevertheless it would be true to say Monty tended to get involved more with works of industrial clients, rather than with monumental city buildings. Monty could always immerse himself within the client's real problems, following and understanding their production processes, and in this way feed in his own appreciation and ingenuity, and so contribute to the overall concept of any scheme.

One such client was Spillers Limited, the great flour-milling and animal-feedstuffs manufacturers, now part of Dalgety plc. Faber was appointed for three of their large projects in the early Romney House days: these were a boon to the firm's survival through the difficult times of the Slump. They were to be constructed at the shipping ports of Cardiff, Avonmouth and Newcastle-upon-Tyne, convenient for the receipt of grain, largely from the North American continent. The three jobs were phased about eighteen months apart, so that whereas design on Cardiff began in the office in 1931, construction on site at Newcastle was not completed until 1937. Each job comprised a silo, a mill-house and a warehouse.

The silos in each case were required to be of different capacity; but as grain silos associated with milling operations have always to be split up into relatively small bins to suit the needs of the miller who blends the grains from different consignments, it was decided to pick on preferred dimensions for a standard bin, and then achieve the required overall capacity for each complex by adopting the appropriate number and configuration of bins of this size. The dimension chosen for the normal bins was 14ft square on plan by 100ft high; and the tonnage requirements were met at Cardiff (30,000 tons) by arranging 75 bins in a plan configuration of 15 x 5, at Avonmouth (25,000 tons) with 68 bins arranged 17 x 4, and at Newcastle (40,000 tons) with 96 bins arranged 16 x 6. The bin walls were 6½ ins thick of reinforced concrete. A floor was provided for the feed-conveyors above the bins, and another floor below for the extract-conveyors.

The construction of the silos on each of these three sites were early cases of the use of sliding shuttering (later to become known as 'slip-form' construction) enabling all the walls for the full 100ft height of the bins to be built in a period of only about ten days. The speed at which the shutters are slid has to be such that the concrete in the upper part of the shutters is plastic enough to offer little resistance to sliding, whilst the concrete emerging at the bottom of the shutters must have set so as to stand firm on its own without slumping. For this reason the engineer needs complete control of the setting-time of the concrete, and this was achieved here by controlling the temperature of the concrete – taking advantage of the fact that the speed at which concrete sets is affected greatly by its temperature. All three slides were carried out in the depth of winter, and plants were installed for warming the concrete materials before and after mixing, so that the temperature of the concrete was at all times under control. This temperature was normally kept at about 60°F, but could be increased if the concrete was setting too slowly in very cold ambient conditions, and *vice versa*. Concreting proceeded in each case with three gangs working eight-hour shifts in continuous procession.

At each of the three sites the juxtaposition of the silos, mill-houses and warehouses is different due to process needs and land space availability. The simplest layout is at Avonmouth where the three buildings stretch out in one logical line behind and parallel to the wharf front, with the silo and receiving house at one end (265ft), with a high-level bridge (75ft) connecting across to the mill-house (225ft), which abuts the warehouse (170ft), forming a complex of total length on the waterfront of 735ft, and height about 100ft except for the silo and receiving house which are respectively 140 and 155ft high. At Newcastle less land space was available, and the mill-house had to be built on top of the warehouse, making for a twelve-storey building 170ft high. Generally the whole of these buildings were constructed in reinforced concrete. An interesting exception was the mill-house at Avonmouth which was of structural steelwork, where 1500 tons were fabricated within five weeks of the date of order and erected complete in a further three-and-a-half weeks – remarkable progress for a seven-storey building 225ft long, 78ft wide and 104ft high.

Due to the weakness of the made ground behind the existing wharf walls, the foundations for each of these jobs were piled. All the piles were 16in square of reinforced concrete, driven with a 4-ton hammer dropping 4ft until the number of blows per foot reached 120. The piles were then considered good for carrying a load of 60 tons each. About 2000 piles were cast and driven at each site: this was to cause the general ground level to rise about nine or twelve inches. At Cardiff and Newcastle the piles were about 40ft long.

At Avonmouth the piles had to be about 70ft long for the following reason. Borings indicated that the made ground extended to a depth of 45ft, where a hard layer of about 10ft thickness was reached. The adjacent dock wall was founded on this hard layer. Below the hard layer came a 15ft thickness of soft clayey material, below which hard red marl was reached at a total depth nearing 70ft. The driving of test-piles showed that what would normally be considered an acceptable set was obtained in the hard layer; but had the piles been terminated here, and the load from the new works transferred to the hard layer (which would have put an additional 3 tons per sq. ft. on the soft material under this layer) there would have been serious risk of the soft layer squeezing and moving bodily out into the dock, taking the dock wall with it, and letting down the hard layer and the whole of the new works. Accordingly Faber had the piles deliberately driven through the hard layer, so as to reach their final set in the hard red marl lower down. This involved very heavy drilling of the piles, which in consequence were made of a richer mix of concrete than normal, and cast at a temperature of about 70°F and carefully protected to maintain this warmth right through the period of curing. It was found these precautions had a very marked effect on the ability of the piles to withstand the heavy driving.

These Spillers jobs were a splendid joint effort between Faber and Monty, and were to lead to other appointments from the same source, notably at Birkenhead, Plymouth, Hull, Cambridge and Gainsborough. The whole of the three works described proved to be extremely economical. The costs per cubic foot (pre-war), exclusive of foundations and M & E services, were

                Silos .... 4d to 5d
                Mills 9d
                Warehouses ..... 6d to 7d

Another industrial project undertaken at this time was the Nine Elms warehouse for the Southern Railway, on the Thames south bank in London, immediately west of Vauxhall Bridge, and by coincidence opposite Dolphin Square, then also in the course of construction. A comparison of the photos of the Spillers job at Avonmouth and the Nine Elms job shows the similarity of aesthetic treatment Faber had given. Faber had become very conscious, early on, of the need for industrial buildings to be pleasing to the eye as well as economical and profit-producing to their owners, particularly when the buildings were large and occupying prominent positions, and he regarded this a part of his responsibility.

At Avonmouth (as indeed also at Cardiff and Newcastle) he had enhanced the appearance of the enormous areas of the silo walls by carrying the dividing bin-walls through to be expressed on the face as vertical piers at 14ft intervals, giving the structure a rhythm and character by the emphasis of such vertical treatment, whilst at the same time indicating its function. The function is further indicated by suitable fenestration of the top and bottom conveyor-floors and of the receiving house at one end, so that the parts where work is done are consciously different from the parts provided for bulk storage. The separation of the top floor from the grain storage is also marked by the set-back at the top of the bins and the change in treatment achieved by stopping the projecting piers at this level. Similar set-backs are provided to the receiving house tower which houses the elevator heads, giving a sense of strength and stability whereby the upper part of the structure looks lighter than the lower, and the silhouette is increased in interest.

Much the same sort of techniques were used on the Nine Elms warehouse, which as a result of its bulk might otherwise have appeared a hard rectangular heap on London's riverside. The interesting silhouette Faber achieved here came from making features of the three towers which house the lift motor-rooms, ventilating fans and water tanks. The function of the building is expressed by the warehouse-doors which give onto the waterside, as well as by the three large cranes corresponding to the three elevator towers. A certain harmony was achieved by making a feature of the cranes rather than seeking to defy or ignore them. On completion, the building was considered worthy of floodlighting, and certainly added to the river scene.

In this happy and most prolific period of his life, Faber was living with his family in a grand home at Kenley known as Hayes Court. Approached by a winding driveway, it stood in a large and splendid garden near the top of a Surrey hill, overlooking London. It was an ideal situation for large parties; and for a number of years Faber used to invite the whole of his staff and families down to a summer garden party. These were delightful occasions, well planned in detail by Faber's wife, Joan, who fulfilled well her part as the caring hostess. Much effort was put into preparing the garden beforehand, so the tennis competition could be fought out in the lower garden by the plum walls, while badminton was being contested within the rose garden above the house, while croquet and putting were available on the front lawn for those of a less hearty persuasion. Some of the guests would arrive by train, and need meeting from the station at the bottom of the hill by the luckier ones who had come by car. Indeed arrivals were the subject of much fun, sometimes leading to shrieks of laughter, seeing what the others looked like away from the office, and what were their wives and girl friends like, and what sorts of dresses did they wear.

White flannels and blazers were the style of the time for the men, and relative prowess on the tennis court used to be a cause of great amusement. Vaughan's play, as with his engineering, stood out well to the fore, with a powerful cannon-ball service no-one could see or comprehend; and through all this achievement Vaughan remained as cool as a cucumber. Faber's methods were more vigorous and exhausting, though, in terms of result, no more successful. Monty's game was only very average, but he was certainly the most entertaining to play with or watch, his running commentaries and explanations keeping everyone including himself doubled in laughter.

When the games were over, my mother had ready a tremendous cold buffet table, including, as a high spot, strawberries and ice-cream – this before the days of home refrigerators. Some of the party would gather in groups in the house sipping their claret cup; others would take a stroll round the garden and enjoy their drinks sitting outside. Then in the evening there would be dancing out on the lawn, lit by fairy-lights strung amongst the large trees. When, late at night, the party was over, some of the cars people had come in would start, and others would not; but under Monty's direction, and with everyone's cooperation and the advantage of the hill, the guests managed, amidst cheers, to get themselves going and back to their homes in readiness for the Monday morning to follow.

It was at this stage that Bob Glover, now in his mid-thirties, was starting to show up in the office as a senior. An extension had been built to Romney House, and the firm spread itself to occupy additional space. The greater elbow-room enabled private 'horse-box' cubicles to be built along one side for the seniors, and Glover was given one of these.

Glover's origins were in the Kent countryside, and this was reflected in his slow thoughtful manner of speech and the comfort and shape of his vowels. Although as a young man he had been a vigorous sportsman, doing well at his school and at college in football, already there were signs of his life-style developing into an almost calculated pattern of shrewd caution remote from any glamour or display. In later years he would say he had never aspired to anything more than contributing the support of a reliable back-room boy. This was a typical dry Glover understatement. It is true that in any engineering problem or business situation, no-one ever saw Glover hurrying his way round corners; on the contrary he would tend to go quietly through mental short-cuts of his own, often being the first to reach the goal. In later years Faber acquired a special respect for Glover as having a 'sound and solid head on those shoulders'.

In 1935 Faber was approached by Brigadier-General Critchley, that great dynamic character, to assemble ideas and draw up a scheme for Harringay Arena, to seat 10,000 spectators for boxing, or 8,000 for ice-hockey, all under one saucer-shaped roof having no internal support that would obscure the view of the action. This was the first major job Faber delegated to Glover to administer. Faber's scheme was an elongated octagonal plan, 320ft by 225ft. The site comprised poor ground, requiring the driving of piles about 50ft long, all the more necessary because of the two tunnels of the Piccadilly underground railway which ran diagonally beneath the stadium. The superstructure for the twenty-four tier stepped seating was of reinforced concrete. The roof was in structural steelwork, and an early experience of long-span construction. The job was built to a tight programme. The first pile was driven in February 1936 and the completed arena staged its first event, an ice-hockey match, in September the same year. Glover always remembered this job with affection and as a special achievement of which he was justly proud.

In its time Harringay Arena served a wide variety of functions. First and foremost it was an ice-hockey stadium, prominent for international and league matches. League teams had colourful names like the Wembley Lions, the Brighton Tigers, the Earls Court Rangers. Harringay was the only rink having two teams – the Harringay Racers and the Harringay Greyhounds – and this had the commercial advantage that when one team was playing away, the other could draw a packed stadium through the turnstiles at home. Then through the Christmas school holidays Harringay used to stage Tom Arnold's international circus, the band for which was conducted by Charlie Shadwell of BBC Variety Orchestra fame, who subsequently became the cheerful landlord of the Green Man pub at Trumpington, Cambridge. Harringay also scored a first with the start of the Horse of the Year Show in 1949, and kept this annual event until 1956 when its popularity outgrew the stadium's seating capacity, and it was shifted to Wembley. Another noteworthy use of Harringay was in 1954 when the American evangelical preacher Dr. Billy Graham filled the Arena with his meetings over a three week period.

Sadly, due to changing times and changing needs, both Harringay Arena and the Nine Elms warehouse were to be demolished after about forty years: 'sadly', because to Faber they had been challenging assignments, where he had had to conceive and manage without any architectural assistance, and in the main – for what these jobs were – had succeeded. Indeed the same was true of the three jobs for Spillers, and the Northolt Stands. These were all jobs Faber had enjoyed greatly. It was Faber's experience in each of these that led him to appreciate and respect all the more the stimulation of collaborating with competent architects. It also led him to present in 1941 his paper to the Civils entitled 'Aesthetics of Engineering Structures' referred to later, following which he was asked to present in 1944 the introductory lecture at the Civils to a series of lectures entitled 'The Aesthetic Aspect of Civil Engineering Design' where the other lecturers included amongst others Professor C. E. Inglis (Past-President I. C. E.) and Professor P. Abercrombie F.R.I.B.A.

The year 1936 was the year of Faber's peak overall performance. He was heavily committed on works with such great architects as Sir Herbert Baker and C. Cowles Voysey; equally he was carrying the jobs for Spillers, Nine Elms and Harringay, and fulfilling the challenging programme set for Dolphin Square: at the same time he produced with Kell the book *Heating and Air-conditioning of Buildings*; and this was the year much of his time was to be taken up by his function as President of the Institution of Structural Engineers. All this he achieved with a total supporting staff of less than forty, including coverage of all administrative, personnel, public relations and business responsibilities. For a man of his zest, who at that stage would always throw himself personally into any commitment he had undertaken, it was a record of extraordinary energy. And just to fill in a few spare evenings he did a 40in by 30in water-colour perspective of the Nine Elms warehouse floodlit by night, and submitted this to the Royal Academy for their Summer Exhibition. It matters not that the selection committee did not accept his painting; he had demonstrated there was no limit to his capacity for trying.

The same year included also the Queen's Hotel, Leeds, for the LMS Railway. This was one of the most modern hotels to be constructed in England at the time, with a frontage of 230ft onto City Square and a height of 120ft above ground level, with kitchens and other services housed in cellars below. The architects were W. Curtis Green & Partners and W. H. Hamlyn. All the bedrooms had mechanical ventilation so that double-glazing could be used and kept shut. This was very necessary in Leeds to exclude the noise from trams and iron tyres and horse-drawn traffic on cobbled streets; also to exclude the dust and grime from an unusually dirty atmosphere with the railway station on one side (steam trains) and a power station on the other. Inlet air came from vertical ducts near the central corridor, and was blown across the bedrooms and drawn out by exhaust ducts from the bathrooms, the bathrooms being internal so as to reserve the outside for bedrooms and windows. Altogether six separate ventilation plants were provided for the building to meet the varying requirements of aspect, temperature and humidity at various times and different occupancy. Thus two served the bedrooms, three the public rooms, and one the kitchens.

Air filtration, for the reasons already given, was a matter of great importance, and the air stream in every plant went first through an oil filter, then through a fabric filter, and finally through a washer. All the washers were provided with glass eliminator plates. Although the fresh-air inlet to the ventilation plant was brought down to the plant chamber in the basement by means of a shaft from a low roof at third-floor level, it was found during the summer to be so highly charged with mosquitoes as to block completely the oil filters. The mosquitoes' wings lay flat against the oily surface and piled up solid. How mosquitoes could have chosen to live in the Leeds atmosphere of those days is difficult to imagine, but it is a fact they did. But for the filters, these mosquitoes would have been discharged into the public rooms and bedrooms alike.

The evening of the gala opening banquet which followed closely the completion of this building was attended by the Princess Royal, the civic dignitaries and all the Railway VIP's. The occasion was rounded off with a grand ball at which the lights were to be dimmed, and a large illuminated swan would cross the ballroom floor while rose petals showered down upon it from the ceiling. These petals were to be dropped through a large central lantern feature which was part of the architectural treatment, and which also had been used as a means of air extraction. The swan duly appeared, propelled across the ballroom by someone inside; but unfortunately its lights weren't working because the plug on its flexible lead had come out. Behind the swan, on all fours, was an electrician in dungarees frantically trying to get the plug in. Meanwhile the man responsible for the showering rose petals was having no luck at all. His hands could be seen desperately throwing the petals down, but as fast as they appeared they were caught in the upward draught of the extract system and pulled out of sight again. Not a single petal reached the unlit swan!

Also at this time came large bulk-store buildings for National Fertilisers Ltd. at Avonmouth. One of these was for the storage of 30,000 tons of phosphate, and was 300ft long, 110ft wide, and 50ft high to the crown. The phosphate material has an angle of repose of approximately 30°, and is introduced to the store on belt conveyors running along the ridge and discharging by means of ploughs at points as desired to form a heap 35ft high. The width of the heap at floor level is controlled by a 10ft height of stanking sloping inwards at 45°. The design of the roof was not without interest. It is clear that if there were no wind or other horizontal forces the most economical structural shape would be a parabola or catenary. When, however, the downward weight is combined with a lateral wind, the line of thrust, instead of forming a pure catenary symmetrical about the centre-line, forms a curve in which the maximum ordinate moves towards the direction from which the wind is coming. Two such lines of thrust were drawn, one for the case of the wind coming from the left, and one for the case of the wind coming from the right. These lines were then made the outlines of steel braced trusses, being the two ribs of a three-pinned arch structure that in consequence had the interesting property that the line of thrust would under no circumstances go outside the limit of the section. It was found on analysis that this design, when compared to others using straight joist sections, gave an economy of steel of approximately sixty per cent; and with fabrication costs as they were at the time, this design was adopted for the lines of the trusses.

The phosphate material weighs approximately 100 lbs per cubic foot so that the maximum pressure it presented on the ground per square foot was 3500lbs, or rather more than $1\frac{1}{2}$ tons. Test loads had indicated that this was much greater than the ground would be able to carry without very considerable settlement; indeed the settlement would probably be in terms of several feet. Such settlement would necessarily be accompanied by the outward spread of the sides of the building, letting down the arched roof construction. Alternatively the arch foundations would have to be tied together by steel rods in the floor, but with the floor settling so much these rods would be distorted to such an extent that the roof would become disfigured quite unpredictably or even caused to collapse. For these reasons the whole floor was piled, the piles needing to be closer together near the middle of the heap where the load was greatest, and further apart nearer the sides. The floor was made 12ins thick of reinforced concrete so as to spread the load of $1\frac{1}{2}$ tons per square foot on to the bearing piles.

Another industrial job of considerable civil-engineering challenge, and very close to Faber's heart, was the rolling-mill at Shotton in 1938, designed to produce continuously a sheet of steel 5 feet wide at a rate of two-thirds of a mile per minute. This was for John Summers & Sons Ltd., later to become part of the British Steel Corporation. The hot-mill and cold-mill buildings were both nearly a third of a mile long, with 100ft span overhead travelling-cranes at 36ft height having carrying-capacities ranging from 15 tons to 50 tons. A strip mill of this character, in which steel billets are rolled down to thin sheet, involves machines subject to enormous impact forces, and the machines themselves have to be held down by foundation bolts as much as 6 inches in diameter and require to be anchored to foundations of very great mass. In many cases these foundations are of extremely intricate construction, accommodating tunnels in which the lubrication and other systems are threaded and housed.

The site selected for the works at Shotton was a large flat area at roughly 14.50ft O.D. level, near the bank of a river. The subsoil consisted of quicksand extending from ground level to a depth of several hundred feet. When simple excavations are attempted in ground of this nature, they fill back on their own accord almost as quickly as the material is taken out. Many of the foundations were necessarily about 100ft square and depth about 16 feet, and the problem was how to construct such foundations in these conditions. Ground de-watering techniques had not yet been developed. The use of sheet-piling to enclose the areas of foundations was considered, but, apart from the great cost and delay which such a method would entail, the long struts which would be required in supporting the sheet-piling and their interference with the construction of the foundations formed serious objections. Furthermore, though sheet-piling would keep the quicksand out at the sides, it would not prevent it from bubbling up at the bottoms in these particular conditions.

Accordingly, it was decided to raise the whole level of the works from 14.50ft to 31.50ft O.D. – a matter of 17 feet – so as to obviate excavation entirely. The foundations were therefore built from marsh-level upwards, and the whole level of the ground was raised to the new ground-level by filling in sand around the foundations after they had been constructed. The foundations were piled with reinforced-concrete piles, and construction of the foundations then proceeded normally above ground, whereby all the previous difficulties were avoided.

The area of sand filling required was 600ft in width and more than a third of a mile in length, to an average thickness of 16 feet. This sand was obtained by suction-dredging from the adjacent river, and delivered as a mixture of sand and water by pumping through large-bore pipes. The sand was left on the site, the water returning to the river. It was anticipated that to excavate this enormous quantity of sand from the river bottom would necessitate frequent moving of the suction-dredger and consequent movement of the delivery-pipes, which would have been costly and time consuming. In the actual event, however, it was found the dredger could be left in one place, and the river conveniently brought fresh sand to the dredger as quickly as it could be disposed of, which rendered the operation much easier and cheaper. Investigation showed this method of overcoming the difficulties of Shotton was by far the

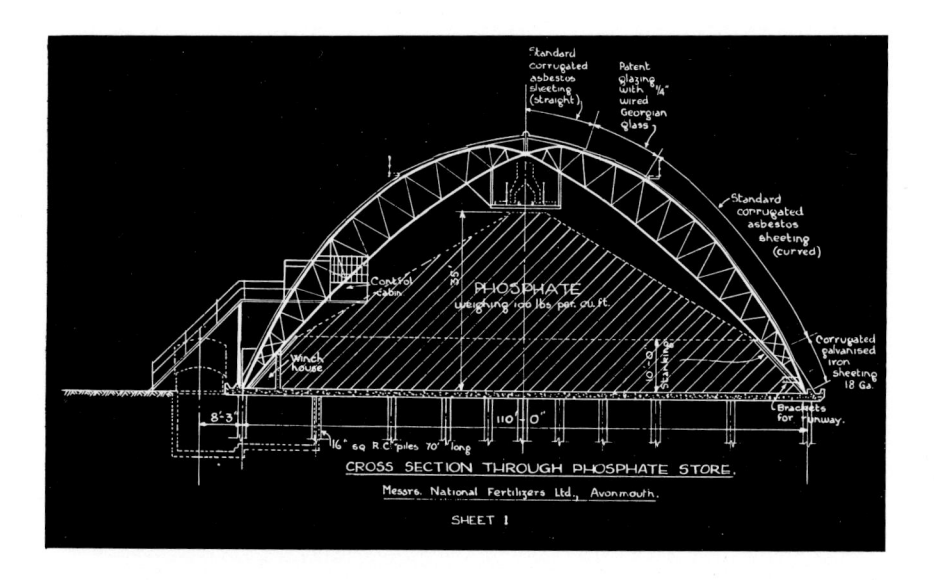

Phosphate store at Avonmouth for National Fertilisers with arch structure of steel braced trusses.

Grain silos, mill and warehouse on the waterfront at Avonmouth for Spillers, now part of Dalgety (mid 1930s).

Nine Elms warehouse for the Southern Railway on the Thames south bank in London (mid 1930s).

Stanley Vaughan (1895–1979).

John Robert Kell (1902–1983).

Part of 240ft span steel roof trusses for sheds at Blackpool for Vickers Armstrongs to assemble and test Wellington aircraft (Wartime).

Phoenix 'A1' units standing in position at Mulberry 'B' – the British harbour at Arromanches, Normandy (Wartime).

Structural steel frame for the rebuilding of the House of Commons (1948).

quickest and cheapest of a number of alternative schemes considered at the time.

Notwithstanding the success of the operations now being administered from Faber's organisation within Romney House, world affairs outside were in a troubled state. In 1935 MacDonald was replaced as Prime Minister by Stanley Baldwin; and in 1937 Baldwin was replaced by Neville Chamberlain. In March 1938 Hitler entered Vienna and took over Austria as part of Germany. Later that year Chamberlain flew to Munich to meet Hitler who was then already threatening to enter Czechoslovakia. When London became aware of this, a general anxiety spread that a European war might not be long delayed, with air-raids on our own cities. A week later Chamberlain flew to Munich again, this time returning with his questionable 'peace in our time' paper. Trenches were now dug in the London parks, and civilian gas-masks issued throughout the country.

In March 1939 Germany did indeed take over Czechoslovakia. The same month it was understood that Hitler was planning to invade Poland. Poland was seeking to maintain some sort of relationship with Germany; but Britain preferred to have Poland as an ally who could, if required, open up a second front against Germany. Accordingly Chamberlain gave Poland a guarantee that Britain would stand by her if Germany attacked.

It had become all too clear another major war was in the offing. When later in the year this was to come about, the Romney House era was to come to an end, as also was the very close personal control Faber had always managed to exercise over the whole of the firm's work and affairs up till that time.

5

The Second World War Period

By the age of fifty, Faber would sometimes drop his guard over finer points of personal behaviour. This is explainable, no doubt, by the enormous pressure of responsibility he was carrying and the burden upon him of the fame he had already won. For example, he might show impatience or disrespect for others less gifted than himself by talking them down; due to pressures on his time he might arrive at business or social gatherings quite unsuitably dressed, to the embarrassment of his host; his behaviour at table might be gauche and clumsy simply because of the need, as he saw it, to get on and be done; his deference, sometimes to those of higher rank, grew unreliable, whether out of ignorance or from his own sense of values not coinciding with normal custom. None of this was doing him any good, and, being a man who would not take kindly to correction from others, there was little could be done for him. Mother would admonish him with good humour and patience, but this only led to added difficulty between them.

This behaviour tended to cause a number of people, nothwithstanding how greatly they respected his ability, to keep from getting too close. Some engineers of lower calibre who had openly been talked down, had no wish for a second instalment; they might well be jealous of Faber's capability, but this would not prevent them speaking critically of him in his absence. This would not be so evident amongst the bigger engineers, as, for example, witnessed earlier in the cases of Sydney Harbour Bridge and the Mersey Tunnel, where two of the finest civil practices came to him for professional assistance. And some architects, whilst wanting his technical competence, did not want to be coerced as to their architecural proposals; indeed they wanted an engineer who would help them realise their aspirations – not one who would argue against them. It would of course depend much on personal chemistries. Not a foot went wrong with Faber's relationship with Sir Herbert Baker over any of the dozen or so fine jobs those two did together; neither of them would suffer fools gladly, and both enjoyed and respected greatly the directness of the other. Faber also got on extremely well with Cowles Voysey, yet there could never have been two men with more different approaches: Voysey always quiet and patient and reserved – Faber with his sense of restless urgency and bold initiative.

Faber's little bursts of unreasonable behaviour would sometimes lead him into moods of loneliness. But here was a vicious circle. Loneliness arose too from his professional ability being so far in advance of that of his contemporaries. Out in the vanguard, so to speak, with an untrodden path before him, he often longed for a friend capable of guiding him, someone of equal brilliance on whose shoulder he might sometimes lean; and this form of loneliness may have been what led him through carelessness to some of his weirder quirks of behaviour.

It was in these moods of loneliness he would turn for solace to music. The composer for whom he had the greatest affinity was Wagner. The *Oxford Companion to Music* describes Wagner as "the boldest composer the world has ever known ... one who believed in his own greatness and inspired others with that belief". In this regard it would be fair to say that as Wagner was to music, so Faber was to his own particular style of engineering; and he was not unaware of the similarity. He believed Wagner's immense four-evening drama *The Ring of the Nibelung* was the most splendid musical creation of all time. When for some years the BBC used to relay the whole of this work on consecutive evenings, Faber would be found in his shirt-sleeves, with the wireless going full blast as he followed the performance through on the full scores spread across the dining-room table, himself desperately conducting the more complicated passages, partly by use of his arms but augmenting this with enthusiastic grunts of encouragement. At the quieter parts he would hold his hands up to his imaginary orchestra, giving gentle 'shush' sounds with arrogant authority.

To watch him enjoy Wagner at Covent Garden was a unique experience. He was completely mesmerised. His moist blue eyes showed he had been spirited away to some dreamland he shared alone with the music. He would be living the part of Wotan, bearing all the anxiety of that character and all the responsibility of the performer. Wotan's nine daughters, the wild horsewomen of the air, the Valkyrie, are, according to Scandinavian mythology, appointed to bear to Valhalla the bodies of their heroes slain in battle. The 'Ride of the Valkyries' would lift Faber from his seat and into the heavens along with these goddesses. When, early in his married life, he had moved from Croydon to Farthing Downs at Coulsdon, his three-bedroomed house had had to be called Valhalla – hall of the valiant, house of the gods.

Later when he bought Hayes Court at Kenley, the family had become close friends with the Watson family at Reedham. Aubrey Watson had his own small but efficient civil-engineering business. The families would share holidays sailing in Norfolk; summer weekends were invariably in and out of one anothers gardens playing tennis. Ella Watson was a charming lady and a competent pianist, and she it was who used to accompany Oscar at her piano as he sang his way through many happy afternoons and evenings. His style of song by now had become more romantic and melancholy than in his school days. "O mistress mine! Where are you roaming?" and – till the tears might easily fall – "I did but see her passing by, And yet I love her till I die". Faber, too, was not unaccomplished at the piano, but here again his escape from everyday cares tended to be a little solemn, a search for peace: "Jesu, joy of man's desiring" and "Where sheep may safely graze".

Another of his musical outlets was his association with the Croydon Music Society. This was a delightful group, but needed pulling together somewhat. Oscar was drawn into the Society by Arthur and Marjorie Webb with whom he had become friendly back in his Croydon days. It was remarkable how, as conductor, he could enliven and co-ordinate the efforts of that orchestra. At the end of a performance, he would turn to the audience and bow modestly, with an amusing querilous expression of some anxiety, almost of apology. It wasn't quite his scene, but he did an excellent job and was much appreciated.

The only period in Faber's life when he really seemed to lose his sense of direction was the year or so before the Second World War. Being a realist, he saw the possibility of Britain being over-run by the Germans. His marriage was not holding together too comfortably, and already at one stage he had thought of living away from home. Then, in the spring of 1939, he decided he would move with his family – never mind their wishes and convenience – to America for some unspecified period, depending on how Europe and things in general might sort themselves out. To safeguard his practice, he had the idea of bringing Jim Vaughan in as a partner, calling the firm Faber Vaughan & Partners, and once the partnership had been launched offering a partnership to Rob Kell. The necessary Deed was drawn up, but Vaughan wanted too many irritating amendments; and so, bit by bit, Faber reappraised the whole situation, and settled down as his usual self once more.

When the War came in 1939, the staff at Romney House had grown to forty-five. About four days before the Sunday of Neville Chamberlain's Declaration of War, Faber decided the firm should evacuate – some North and some South – and a proportion worked in three rather scruffy little houses in St. Albans (Worley Road and Church Crescent), while the remainder moved into Faber's home at Hayes Court in Kenley. Faber moved his family to a new house at Kingswood, about six miles further out (it was on a Costain housing estate – which explains how he got it at about six hours notice!) Subsequently, one night in 1940, the mounting and immediate action of a Naval pom-pom, unheralded, in a field only about 200 yards away was interpreted as "things getting rather hot", and Dr. and Mrs. Faber, who by then were living on their own, packed and moved to Hertfordshire the next morning, where they lived in Harpenden as PGs until later they were able to find a permanent home at Chatley Dene in Rothamstead Avenue. Here they remained and saw their lives through together. With Faber no longer in Surrey there was no purpose of maintaining a staff at Hayes Court; nevertheless a proportion of the firm's pre-war records were left there, and these together with the buildings later went up in flames one night in an incendiary air attack.

Thus Faber settled down to work for the next fifteen years – almost to his end – in a poor semi-detached house in Church Crescent in St. Albans. These working circumstances never bothered or depressed him in the least. He would motor in each morning, and, being now somewhat portly, reverse his car in the mirror with varying results, spread a rug over the bonnet and hold it in place by sample bricks kept for the purpose, trundle up the much worn stone steps into the little house, and there start his long and busy day. His firm's contribution to the war effort was enormous, including work for the War Office, the Admiralty, the Ministry and Supply and the Ministry of Aircraft Production, amounting altogether to about £25 million of engineering works within the much greater total value of the projects as a whole. When one realises what the pound was worth in those days, it makes the mind fairly boggle. What a pity it is so much of the fees from all that went straight into paying the enormous Surtax charges on one individual – how much more praiseworthy and sensible it would have been if he had shared the rewards more widely amongst his staff who were then working seven long days a week with practically no holidays. But somehow Faber always felt he was achieving something special for himself by paying people less than they were really worth to him; inevitably of course the effect was that over the years many promising members of staff drifted away, so increasing the burden of responsibility at the top of the firm, as also subsequently the problems of succession.

One common feature of all the wartime jobs was their sheer size. The problem was always to get the greatest amount of construction achieved in the least possible time. Thus, management and organisation often figured as much as elegance or originality of engineering. There was no longer the cream of the country's craftsmen and labour available to draw upon, so that as far as possible simplicity had to be the order of the day.

Outstanding of the firm's works at this time were the three Royal Ordnance filling factories at Risley, Kirkby, and Ruddington; the Magnesium Electron Ltd. metal production factory at Padiham; the Metal & Produce Recovery Dept. plants at Eaglescliffe and Cowley; the large-span aircraft assembly-sheds at Windermere, Belfast and Blackpool; and the Mulberry Harbour Scheme for the Normandy invasion. How so much could have been handled from a base in three small houses in St. Albans is of course explained by the fact that many of Faber's senior people were out resident on the jobs they were handling, with their own staffs specially recruited and working on site. For example, Jim Vaughan, who ran the Royal Ordnance Factory job at Kirkby in Lancashire, had his own civil and structural staff of about seventy, and M & E staff of some twenty under Rob Kell's continuous visiting supervision, plus all the necessary admin staff of accountants, secretaries and the like, making a total team of up to about a hundred.

The Kirkby job comprised amongst other things more than 800 separate buildings of all sizes and degrees of intricacy, many mounded all round to full height to limit the effects of any explosion (by accident or enemy action); over twenty miles of railway with extensive eight-leg sidings and connection to the main line, nearly twenty miles of heavy-duty roadways, numerous road-over-rail bridges and level-crossings, two sizeable reservoirs, and a comprehensive district heating scheme including three boiler houses with nine Lancashire boilers in each, and miles of steam mains slung up on concrete posts covering the whole site. The peak labour force was over 15,000 men. Inevitably there were those dreadful great site meetings where members from each of the administrative, engineering, architectural and quantity-surveying teams were present along with representatives from all the firms of contractors, sub-contractors and suppliers. These went on for hours and hours – seemed like days – until the only remedy at the end was to retire elsewhere for liquid refreshment as a solace to one's spirits.

One of the more challenging fields of structural design was for large-span sheds for the assembly and servicing of military aircraft. For Short Brothers two such sheds of 300ft clear span were constructed, one at Windermere and one at Belfast, both carrying tracks for 20-ton overhead underslung travelling-cranes. For Vickers Armstrongs at Blackpool three sheds were constructed each of 240ft clear span, and each provided with tracks to carry six 5-ton overhead cranes. These roofs were early examples of the use of high-tensile steel (Ducol) on such a scale, and were designed at St. Albans by Faber and Monty.

The principal works unit at Blackpool comprised one large continuous factory building nearly a quarter of a mile square producing *ipso facto* its own problem in terms of ventilation. Kell solved this for the general working area by the provision of seven main fresh-air inlet plants (four at the west end and three at the east end), each feeding one long horizontal duct at roof level about 35ft above the working floor, each duct extending about two-thirds the length of the whole factory, tapering down from 7ft diameter at the plant end to 2ft 6in at the remote end. Inlet nozzles arranged at intervals along the ducts were of similar design to the ones developed for the Earls Court Exhibition Centre, with facility for directional adjustment and damper control. Extract was by numerous independent extract units spaced uniformly about the roof area.

Meanwhile Faber had his own pet projects which he liked to involve himself in very personally. For example, when the horror of the U-boat blockade had been most pronounced, Faber had conceived the idea of a reinforced concrete floating island anchored in mid-Atlantic as a base from which the convoys of merchant shipping might be better protected. He had no doubt of the practicability of his proposal; but he was not in a position of sufficient influence to be able to persuade or argue successfully the priority he felt such a scheme deserved. But later, in 1943, when the large scale planning for the invasion of Northern France was in progress, problems arose in connection with the Mulberry Harbours where he was able to contribute his talent for designing reinforced-concrete work subject to hydrodynamic effects.

The invasion force with its men, vehicles, armour, ammunition, fuel and other stores would need proper sheltered off-loading facilities in several square miles of protected harbour conditions. Whatever harbour facilities were already standing available on the other side of the Channel would certainly have been well enough mined, fortified and manned to enable the Germans to hamper and cause delay; meanwhile Rommel's troops lying further back could be directed in a matter of days to resist whatever early Allied landings might be achieved, and repel these before proper footholds with adequate back-up of men and supplies could be established. It was decided therefore that the landings should be in great force, and so sited that the apparent unsuitability of their location to receive shipping would take the Germans by surprise. This could only be done if the invasion force took with itself a complete harbour system, capable of having traffic rolling into France as quickly as Rommel could bring up his major defence reserves from behind. At the Quebec Conference in September 1943 it was decided to construct the 'Mulberry' harbours, on the shallow beaches between Cherbourg and Le Havre: the method to be a combination of floating breakwaters ('Bombardons'), blockships ('Gooseberries'), and reinforced concrete caissons ('Phoenixes'). The two main harbours known as Mulberry 'A' and Mulberry 'B', would comprise mainly Phoenixes: the other three would be made up of Gooseberries. Faber flew by night to attend the Quebec Conference, lying in the belly of a Lancaster bomber. He commented afterwards he had 'been frozen so stiff he had doubted whether he would ever thaw out again'.

A great champion for the floating-breakwater idea was Commander Robert Lochner. The scheme was to spread protective chains of such breakwater-units roughly parallel to the coast and about a mile and a half out. Altogether about 3 miles of floating-breakwater would be required. The thinking behind such a device is based on the knowledge that the waves of the sea are relatively skin deep, and any reflecting mass needs to extend from the surface a depth of only about 15 to 20 per cent of the wave-length. The floating wall then needs anchoring to remain relatively stationary, and its natural period of oscillation needs to be considerably longer than the maximum periodicity of the longest wave. Lochner's first prototype was an assembly of rubberised canvas envelopes making a unit 200ft long with 12ft beam and 16½ft draught. This flexible sausage-balloon monster, with its buoyancy characteristics varying according to the configurations of the sea surface, was to be the fickle support for the solid reflecting mass of its reinforced-concrete keel. This keel, weighing 700 tons, was designed by Faber. Three of these 'soft' prototypes – code name appropriately 'Lilo' – were launched and tested in 1943, and proved without doubt the efficacy of Lochner's method: they were found to reduce the heights of waves by 50 per cent. However, because of criticism that the rubberised canvas of Lilo was vulnerable to sharp objects floating in the water and to enemy attack, it was subsequently decided to go from the 'soft' sausage breakwater to a 'hard'-type hollow steel unit of Maltese Cross profile, 200ft long and 25ft high and 25ft wide, the upper limb being watertight to give buoyancy whilst the other limbs were open to allow the sea-water in and so provide the necessary mass. In the event of the landings, the steel breakwaters were found to produce certain hazards to the Allies that quite probably would not have arisen if the Lilo idea had been retained.

The Phoenix concrete caissons for Mulberries 'A' and 'B' were to be towed across the Channel and, when in position, flooded and sunk on the sea bed as a continuous massive wall parallel to the coast and about a mile out, with the return ends of the harbours formed by further Phoenixes linking the main outer lines back to the shore. The outer Phoenixes were to stand mainly in about 5 fathoms of water, and for this depth had to be 60ft high, and for stability, 56ft wide: these were known as the 'A1' units. In shallower water, as at the return ends, the heights of the units were progressively reduced down to 25ft, as also the widths to suit. However all the Phoenixes were approximately the same length – 200ft – and of simple rectangular form, save only their 'swim-ends'. Apart from simplicity of construction, swim-ends have the advantage over pointed bows of giving the steadiest tow and causing the least resistance. Altogether 6 miles of Phoenix caissons were to be ready by D-Day, which turned out to be 6th June 1944 – yet at the end of September 1943 work on their design had not even begun.

Design was by a committee of consulting engineers in liaison with the War Office and Ministry of Supply. The bottoms and external walls, designed for a 20ft head of water – just more than half a ton per square foot, – were to be 15ins thick, with stiffening cross-walls and one central longitudinal division wall 9in thick. The caissons were open at the top. Construction was let out to a number of civil engineering and building contractors, who variously came under the control of seven practices of consulting engineers. Faber handled four firms of contractors, of whom Messrs. Costain, Messrs. Demolition & Construction and Messrs. Nuttall each constructed four of the sixty largest A1 units, i.e. between them a total of twelve, being one fifth of all the A1's – almost half a mile of caissons 60ft high (roughly the height of seven-storey blocks of flats). All this in a period of six months.

However the committe-design had been based on constructing the caissons in dry-docks, or dried out wet docks, or on slipways for side launching: and such facilities as were available in Britian fell far short of meeting the whole of this requirement. Consequently it was arranged that some of the Phoenixes should be built using the basin method for constructing the lower parts: these would then be floated out into deeper water where they could be completed alongside quays. The basins Faber had were all situated in the banks of the Thames: but due to high-tide ground water these could not be excavated more than 8ft deep, with the effect that only 14ft of the total 60ft height could be constructed before floating out. Now the swim-ends, referred to earlier, comprise – in rough and ready terms – a chamfer 20ft by 20ft fore and aft at the bottoms of each unit; so that floating out in only 8ft of water, the concentration of weight in the ends of the caisson coupled with the loss of buoyancy beneath the upswept ends would produce a very considerable hogging moment over the length of the caisson – as yet only 14ft deep, – and would indeed have broken its back. Faber was quick to draw attention to this, as a result of which all units floated out at 14ft height of construction had a considerable quantity of extra reinforcing bars built into the tops of the longitudinal walls as at the 14ft stage. Then after floating, each further 4ft lift of concrete

THE SECOND WORLD WAR PERIOD

construction would – for the same reason – produce additional hogging stresses, and these had to be kept out of the freshly placed concrete: this was done by balancing these additional hogging moments by sagging moments produced by flooding of the amidships compartments of the Phoenixes at all subsequent stages of construction. Finally, in the last concrete pour at the tops of the units, a further band of extra longitudinal steel was built in; after which the unit could be pumped out for greater lightness in towing.

On D-Day, the Gooseberries were the first to cross the Channel, and be manoevred into place and sunk. The same day, the first Bombardons left Britain under tow, and within a week two miles had been assembled off the French coast, the remainder being in place only a few days later. For the first fortnight the Gooseberries and the Bombardons provided practically the whole of the sheltered water available for the invading armies and for the arrival and sinking in position of the Phoenix caissons at Mulberries 'A' and 'B'. Towing of the Phoenixes began the day after D-Day, and about sixty out of a hundred and forty had been placed in position within a fortnight. A freak four-day storm then blew up of force about twice that which had been considered to be the maximum in which it would be practical to carry out the invasion operation at all. Mulberry 'A' suffered the worst from this storm: however at Arromanches, the Mulberry 'B' was successfully completed very close to the original design intentions, and provided two square miles of sheltered harbour conditions. The Mulberry harbours reached a peak capacity about the end of July, when more than 10,000 tons was going through per day. Although the Mulberries were only planned for use over a period of three months, the Arromanches harbour was actually kept in service until late Autumn 1944.

It was at this latter stage of the war, when the strains of heavy responsibility and long working weeks were having their effects, that Vaughan chose to write to Faber giving notice of his intention to leave Faber's firm. Faber had become so wrapped up in his own work, he rarely had the time or the inclination to go round taking much interest in what others were doing. Vaughan resented this, partly because of the great load he personally had been carrying for Faber throughout the war whilst yet only a senior member of staff (it was still Faber's sole practice, with no time for the reappearance of any partnership proposal), and partly because of certain impatiences Faber was expressing or inferring from time to time. It is known there were a number of problems Vaughan would very much have liked the opportunity of discussing and sharing with Faber, but Faber saw no reason why Vaughan should not be self-sufficient to the extent of solving all problems on his own jobs.

Vaughan was up North on the MPRD job at Eaglescliffe, Co. Durham, when he sent in his resignation. Faber reacted by inviting

Vaughan to come to St. Albans to discuss the matter. Vaughan agreed, though he was adamant nothing would deflect him in his resolve now to leave the firm and be free to consider setting up separately on his own. When they met Faber expressed deep sorrow at Vaughan's decision, which perhaps had arisen from overwork and stress: certainly he would make whatever amends Vaughan felt appropriate, if only they could patch up whatever differences there were between them. When Vaughan said this would be quite impossible, Faber asked why. Here Vaughan made what in retrospect he recognised as a most unfortunate mistake: he described to Faber every fault he had known in the man. Faber apparently listened with great interest and asked Vaughan to go on. When at long last Vaughan had finished, Faber apologised profusely, assured Vaughan none of these lapses would recur, and begged Vaughan not to leave him. Vaughan weakened, and withdrew his notice; and for the remainder of Faber's life, the relationship between the two men was so chill that, as far as possible, they kept well clear of one another. Faber's personal respect of Vaughan waned; curiously though, right through to the end of his long life, Vaughan always appeared to retain a great admiration and affection for the memory of Faber.

Faber had many civilian tasks to occupy his mind during these later stages of the War. One of these was the preparation of a feasibility study for the airport later to become known as Heathrow. In 1944, General Critchley, recently appointed as Director-General of British Overseas Airways Corporation, was concerning himself over a site and plant for an airport from which to operate Britain's post-war airlines. Already his old colleague from the GRA days, Lord Brabazon, was applying himself to what was clearly going to be an entirely fresh dimension of civil aircraft, necessitating runways and terminal buildings of a scale hitherto undreamed of. Critchley had the brilliant idea of siting all this on the large flat area of land $12\frac{1}{2}$ miles west of Hyde Park Corner. The space was larger by 10 per cent than America's Idlewild Airport then being constructed 16 miles from New York. In his Memoirs in 1961 entitled 'Critch' he wrote:

> "When the idea was first accepted, I got Oscar Faber, one of the finest civil engineers in the country (he rebuilt the Bank of England, and was responsible for the Mulberrys of D-Day), to draw up an overall plan for this new airport. I won't dwell on this, except to say that it was much superior to the lay-out of the airport that we now have. The cost was estimated at about £8,000,000 which included a large hotel and a railway coming from the Feltham direction. Faber particularly said that there

THE SECOND WORLD WAR PERIOD

should be no tunnelling, as the water level came to within five or six feet of the surface and it would therefore be like tunnelling through a river, and most expensive. Now the cost of the present London Airport, to date, is reported to be in excess of £26,000,000 and it is said that there is a least two miles of tunnelling. When I consider the hotch-potch that London Airport is today I think with regret of the clear-cut plan outlined by Faber."

Another civilian task Faber was faced with at this time concerned that part of the Palace of Westminster which had been destroyed in an air-raid in 1941 including particularly the House of Commons. In December 1943 a Select Committee was set up to collect information and make recommendations. Sir Giles Gilbert Scott was called upon to provide plans and advise on the architecture; and Faber was invited to submit a scheme for the heating, air-conditioning and other M & E servies. The report from the Select Committee published in October 1944 stated:

"The system of heating and ventilation incorporated in Your Committee's plan appears to be the best which modern science can devise.... The plan is ahead of anything which has yet been attempted."

It then referred the House to the fuller wording of Dr. Faber's own report, which included the following:

"In the old House all the air was introduced through gratings in the floor and exhausted through the roof so that the main air-flow was vertically upwards. This is an unnatural system and does not conform to anything in nature, where air currents are horizontal rather than vertical.
"In the old House the vertical system had the disadvantage that any dirt or dust carried in by Members' feet was inevitably either discharged through the gratings or left on the carpet which covered them, and in either case became incorporated in the uprising air currents, which were vitiated thereby."

Faber had added wryly that in those days most traffic in London had been horse-drawn, but this observation did not get into the Report. He had realised also that warm air issuing through the gratings would cause evaporation from Members' feet and so create a sense of coldness; and the greater the complaints from this, the more the air-flow and heat would be increased, so producing the very conditions conducive to hot heads and cold feet. He couched this in respectful terms, saying:

"We aim at producing conditions approximating to those on a fine spring day out of doors, tending to produce

(a) Cool heads and warm feet, and not vice-versa.
(b) Refeshing variable air currents, mostly horizontal in direction."

In 1944 Faber became President of the Institution of Heating and Ventilating Engineers. He held this office for two years, necessitating the delivery of two Addresses, both of which he kept strictly to technical material. The first of these was on National Heating Problems and District Heating. Then in 1946 he addressed the Institution of Mechanical Engineers on The Value of Heat with Special Reference to the Heat Pump. In 1947 he addressed the Civils on Panel Heating. This clearly was the period he was feeling most at home with the M & E side of his work. He was back at the IHVE again in 1951 giving a mammoth paper jointly with Kell on the Heating and Air Conditioning of the House of Commons: he had not long before done one at the Structurals entitled 'Construction of the New House of Commons'. And so his flair for study, descriptive writing and speaking went on year after year. In 1955 his research tests on the enhanced strength of steel pillars when encased in sound concrete was gathered together in a paper 'More Rational Design of Cased Stanchions', and presented at a Structurals' meeting so large in attendance it had to be held in the Conference Room at the Piccadilly Hotel.

Perhaps the most valuable of the papers he prepared at this sort of time were two to the Civils – 'Aesthetics of Engineering Structures' (in 1941) and 'A New Piling Formula' (in 1947). The Aesthetics paper won for him the Baker Gold Medal, and was much referred to for decades to follow; the Piling paper, however, had a hostile reception, though it is undeniable this record of twenty years tests and researches threw much additional light on what has always been an elusive problem lending itself to no precise solution.

In his paper on Aesthetics, Faber said:

"Engineers must conform to the reasonable demand that our cities shall be built with considerations of beauty and harmony, and that engineering structures, forming as they do, important elements in our civilization, must conform to the same requirements and be things of beauty.

"Certain it is that if engineers were to lose a proper appreciation of this essential requirement of their work, or if the younger members of the profession should be brought up in ignorance of it, the public would remove from the control of such engineers the design of important engineering structures."

Referring then to the earliest bridges consisting of trees dragged across a river, he unfolds his argument that the essential requirements for an engineering structure must be to

1. Fulfil all its functional requirements.
2. Be sufficiently permanent.
3. Be reasonably economical.
4. Give aesthetic satisfaction.

To meet the latter requirement, a structure must be satisfactory in

Harmony;
Composition;
Character;
Interest;

and in enlarging on these, he suggested 'interest' to a structure could include

(a) The expression of function.
(b) The expression of construction.
(c) Rhythm.
(d) Texture and colour.
(e) The silhouette.

He then went on, with a supplementary paper, to give examples of how he felt some of these points had been met by his own designs for the Nine Elms warehouse for the Southern Railway on the Thames, and the Silos, Mills and Warehouses for Spillers at Cardiff, Avonmouth and Newcastle.

The Aesthetics paper was entirely convincing, and couched in clear modest terms. No one could deny the desirability of having large structures looking as pleasant as possible; nor had it been difficult to pick upon examples of previous structures where clearly no great consideration had been given to appearance, as for example Charing Cross railway bridge. The Piling paper, on the other hand, was quite a different kettle of fish. After twenty years wrestling with the problem, and having undoubtedy made considerable progress, Faber demonstrated a careless overconfidence, making excessive claim for his own pile-driving formula and unnecessarily hard criticism of Mr. Alfred Hiley's contribution to the subject twenty years before, without himself having seen his own work through to a polished conclusion. Indeed, at the time of going to press, realising how long-winded the whole thing had become, he wrote a much clearer five-page *resumé* which he pinned to the front and called 'Introduction': and in presenting the paper to an expectant Institution audience he tacked on at the end a hastily prepared dissertation of 'Efficiency of blow'.

As a result of these defects, the discussion which followed centred on harsh criticism, rather than recognising the value of what Faber had put forward that was fresh. Perhaps his hope of finding a formula to relate the dynamic performance of driving a pile, to the static load the pile will carry subsequently, was somewhat akin to setting a blind man in a dark room to look for a black hat that wasn't there: but Faber was rather claiming he had found it! In his reply to the discussion he observed bitterly

> "that a paper presented by him to the Institution in 1927 on 'Plastic Yield, Shrinkage, and Other Problems of Concrete', had been derided by nearly every contributor to the discussion upon it (but not by the late Professor W. C. Unwin, Past President of the Institution); yet it was accepted today as common knowledge."

Notwithstanding the cruel experience of this rebuff, when – a year later – Faber heard Miss E. T. Unwin, niece of his great champion W. C. Unwin (1838–1933), had bequeathed a sum to the Institution to be invested in trust for the foundation of a 'William Cawthorne Unwin Lectureship' consisting of an 'Unwin Memorial Lecture' on engineering research, he dived straight in to deliver the Inaugural Unwin Lecture in 1948. Such was the great heart and resilience of the man. The lecture he delivered that wintry evening was warm and perfectly splendid.

> "Among the many totally undeserved honours which have come my way there is perhaps none that I value more than to have been given the opportunity of delivering the first Unwin Memorial Lecture in memory of my old Professor and friend, for Unwin was a remarkable and outstanding man, not only in his own personality but also in the part he played in changing British Engineering from rule-of-thumb methods to methods dependent on the scientific research and understanding of the stresses involved."

Such a generous tribute to a fine old friend was not at all untypical of Faber, yet how different from the insensitive slating he had given poor Hiley, quite unnecessarily, only a year before. This unpredictability of manner came to be recognised generally as one of the great man's quirks – sometimes to the extent of being almost laughable. In a way it was seen by those of us who were closest to him as a rather loveable feature – so long as you remembered and were mentally nimble enough to leap out of the way smartly when the need arose.

6

Into Partnership

The Ground Force Commander of the army in Normandy from June 1944 was General Montgomery, acting under the supreme command of General Eisenhower. Montgomery's command covered two army groups; and all these troops and their equipment and supplies were landed in France through the Mulberry harbours described earlier. By September 1st the Seine had been crossed, and Eisenhower, having now established his forward H.Q. in Normandy, assumed direct command of all land forces. The same day Montgomery was promoted to Field Marshal.

The Rhine was reached in early March 1945, and crossed a fortnight later. Thereafter Montgomery thundered to reach the Baltic at Lubeck and Wismar on May 2nd in time to seal off Schleswig Holstein and the Danish peninsular just six hours ahead of the arrival of the Russians. The Danes have every cause to be eternally grateful for this. On May 3rd Field Marshal Keitel sent a delegation of senior German officers to Montgomery at his Tac HQ at Luneburg Heath, south-east of Hamburg, to sue for peace. Montgomery demanded nothing less than Keitel's authority for them to sign an instrument of unconditional surrender of all German armed forces in North-West Germany, Holland and Denmark. This they did on May 4th, whereupon Montgomery ordered the official cease-fire for May 5th. On May 7th, back at Eisenhower's headquarters, the Germans signed the instrument of total unconditional surrender on all fronts; and this was ratified at Marshal Zhukov's Russian HQ in Berlin on May 8th. The European War was at an end.

Back in Britian not everything could be switched off and turned back to civilian life just like switching off a tap. For one thing, the war against Japan was expected to continue another eighteen months, though, in the event, following the dropping by the Americans of atomic bombs on Hiroshima and Nagasaki, the

Japanese were to surrender after only three more months. For another, many wartime undertakings had to be run down and seen through, as for example the Metal & Produce Recovery Dept plant at Eaglesclffe, and the aircraft factory at Blackpool which was in process of being converted for the mass production of prefabricated aluminium houses.

Faber, in fact, was faced with a three-pronged dilemma. First, there was the need to gather together his senior staff scattered about the country. Second, he was faced with the limited capacity of the three houses in St. Albans, and the unsuitability of their small and ill-lit rooms. Thirdly, what work would there be in the post-war period he could get himself involved in, which would get the practice rolling again in anything like the way it had been in the pre-war Romney House days. At VE Day, the outlook facing Faber was grim indeed.

Then came the good news that the Report on the heating, air-conditioning and other engineering services for the rebuilding of the House of Commons was accepted, and the Ministry of Works wished Faber to act as engineer for these. Sir Giles Gilbert Scott and Mr. Adrian Scott were appointed by the Ministry as architects for the new building, and Faber was appointed by the architects to act as engineer for the structural work too. This was the second great National building of monumental class to be constructed in London in Faber's lifetime – the first being the Bank of England – and Faber was again to be the engineer. Whereas for the Bank the original appointment had been for the civil and structural work, with the services engineering following on as a consequence; for the House of Commons the emphasis had been reversed – the structure being tagged on as a result of the Services Report. The influence of Kell's weight was showing in a very positive way.

The detailed design work for the rebuilding of the House of Commons was done in somewhat Pickwickian accommodation Faber took in the shape of two Solicitors' Chambers on the second floor of 4 Verulam Building in Grays Inn, only a stone's throw from Scott's office in Field Court. This was convenient for working through the intricate details of the job. Vaughan took control of the structural work; and J. R. Harrison (Dick) handled the M & E services work with visiting guidance from Kell who remained based at St. Albans.

The House of Commons is a building contained within the Palace of Westminster. It is not visible from the outside, either on the land or river side, since other buildings of the Palace intervene. The Palace was originally built on a swamp, and part of the site was reclaimed from the River Thames. The level of the sub-basement floor is about 10ft below mean high-tide level. The older building was frequently flooded and "men did row in wherries in the midst of it". In 1579 fish were found dead on the floor. The old building had of course been constructed of stone and brick, and this had been founded on a raft 5ft thick constructed of lime concrete which sat on a 14ft thickness of water-logged sand and gravel which in turn overlaid the blue clay.

Faber did not wish to puncture through this raft and sit independently on the water-logged gravel; yet the friable condition of the lime concrete caused him to limit the pressure on the old raft from his new steel stanchions to 6 tons per sq. ft. This he achieved by cutting local recesses into the raft with 45° slopes to form inverted truncated pyramids, and then concreting individual pad bases within the recesses, so providing the necessary spread without weakening the raft too seriously. The tops of the pad bases were kept far enough below the top of the raft to enable the bloom bases of the structural steel stanchions, sitting on the pads, also to be accommodated within the raft thickness. It was a clever and economical solution, enabling the architects to plan two fine floors for the accommodation of Members' Rooms, Committee Rooms and Minister's Rooms below the floor of the Chamber of the House – which space previously had all been taken up by the old and inefficient heating apparatus.

The main engineering feature of the House of Commons was the air-conditioning of the Chamber itself and the two Division Lobbies. The problem was to maintain a desirable temperature and humidity in the House under extremely varying conditions. At one moment this relatively small Chamber might be almost unoccupied, and then suddenly contain nearly a thousand occupants, all giving off body-heat and moisture – whilst the temperature of the outside air which is used for the ventilation might in the winter be as low as 25°F, and in the summer as much as 85°F. Clearly when the heat of the occupants and the lighting is added to the temperature of the incoming air, summer conditions without refrigeration would be intolerable. Actually, with the nine air-changes per hour provided, the heat generated within the Chamber raises the temperature of the incoming air by 13°F, so that in summertime to achieve an internal temperature of say 70°F, the outside air has to be cooled from 85°F to 57°F; and at the same time the humidity of the air has to be reduced very considerably. In winter, on the other hand, the outside air at 25°F needs heating to raise its temperature by about 45°F, which lowers its relative humidity to such an extent that, for comfort, moisture has to be added in the form of vapour in the plants.

The complication of controlling the plants which condition all this air is dealt with automatically as far as possible by thermostats, but such corrective instrumentation cannot meet the needs of special circumstances, as for example when a large increase in population may occur very suddenly when it becomes known a prominent Member is about to speak. On such occasions the temperature of the incoming air needs to be lowered; but with nine air-changes per hour, it takes nearly seven minutes for the air from the inlets to get through the Chamber, and a further time-lag results from the time taken for the controls to operate, and for the changed air-temperature in the ducts to reach the Chamber. To meet these circumstances, a periscope is installed, whereby the engineer in the control-room in the basement of the building can gauge and anticipate the change of population in the Chamber by watching through a telescopic lens hidden in the carving in the Chamber ceiling. Manual control has also to be relied upon at the times of Divisions, when the Members leave the Chamber for a short period and crowd into the Division Lobbies; on these occasions the cooling air which normally serves the lower portion of the Chamber has to be diverted into the Lobbies.

The difficulty of air-conditioning successfully a Chamber so congested, and so complicated by galleries of varying populations at both ends and along both sides, is not generally appreciated. As a check, a scale model one quarter full-size was constructed by the N.P.L. and subjected to many tests with air introduced at the intended design speeds to determine whether the nine air-changes per hour would lead to excessive local air-movements anywhere. A full-scale model of a 30ft length of the Chamber was then constructed at the Earls Court Exhibition Centre, with tubular electric-heaters simulating the heat of the occupants; and this test also yielded valuable information. Six weeks before the first sitting of the House was due, 400 Guards from Caterham occupied the floor of the Chamber as a practical test, as a result of which it was decided to make considerable modifications to the delicacy of response of the automatic controls. Four days later, the Guards were back again, this time 950 of them, occupying the floor and all the galleries, from which test further adverse effects of body heat showed up necessitating material adjustments to the direction of blow of some of the air. Eighteen days later 950 civil servants occupied the Chamber enabling rather more delicate ajustments to be made, the civil servants radiating less heat and breathing out less moisture than the Guards! At this time only about three weeks remained before the official opening of the Chamber; and further tuning of the system was done using tubular electric-heaters instead of drafting in further persons.

At the first sitting in the Chamber in October 1950, Winston Churchill sat restless in the moving air for some time with his jacket collar turned up. After a while he left, and returned later wearing an overcoat and carrying a rug which he wrapped round his feet. "It's like the bridge of a destroyer in a storm," it is believed he growled to his colleagues on the Front Bench. Soon the necessary adjustments were made to the controls. In 1951 Faber was awarded the CBE for his work in connection with the new building.

Working on the House of Commons enhanced for Faber his great reputation as the total engineer of prestige buildings, and was undoubtedly a factor contributing to the firm's subsequent appointments for such buildings as Lloyds of London in the City; Barclays Bank Head Office, also in the City; the Royal College of Surgeons in Lincoln's Inn Fields, as also the Imperial Cancer Research Building there; and English Electric House (now Citibank's London Headquarters) on the site of the old Gaiety Theatre in Aldwych. To some extent this reputation was a two-edged sword, giving to some the impression of 'gold-plate' and extravagence – a bogey not finally dispelled until in the late fifties when the firm was doing exciting skyscraper buildings in Nigeria, and the very modern Texas Instruments Ltd's factory at Bedford in England. These jobs are described later on.

The appointment for the Royal College of Surgeons was received in 1948. The architect was Alner Hall, an old friend with whom Faber had worked continuously from the early twenties on the building of The Middlesex Hospital, and subsequently its various modifications and extensions. Also by this time, a whole host of jobs of an industrial nature had come in, largely for long-standing clients going back well before the war such as Pinchin Johnson & Co. Ltd. at Poplar and Silvertown (later to become the International Paint Co. Ltd.); Siemens Bros. Ltd. at Woolwich and other centres (later to become part of AEI Ltd., and subsequently GEC Ltd.); and Pirelli General Cable Works Ltd., mainly at Southampton. Fresh industrial clients appeared too; these included the Derby & Midland Mills Ltd., and Clarnico Ltd. the sweet manufacturers, later part of the Trebor Group Ltd. Also by 1948 Faber had started working on the stores and office buildings he was doing for the United Africa Company in the Gold Coast.

Immediately post-war a somewhat specialist field of work was developing and expanding within the firm. This was the heating of the vast spaces within cathedrals. The usual method that had been adopted in Victorian times was to construct open ducts in the centre of the gangways between rows of pews, cover these with cast-iron gratings, run several lengths of cast-iron mains in the ducts, and connect these to cast-iron boilers. Persons coming in from the outside then had no option but to walk on the gratings, which were sometimes noisy, but in any case formed receptacles for any dirt carried in on their boots. This dirt, falling on the heating pipes, tended to get taken up with the uprising hot air, so vitiating the atmosphere. When the spaces between the pipes were small, the dirt would bridge across between the pipes, so diminishing their heating effectiveness. But the greatest disadvantage was that by inducing uprising currents of hot air in the centre of the cathedral, and making no provision for dealing with down-draughts from the very high windows, a circulation was set up in the direction which exacerbated the latter.

Kell had learned something of all this in his earlier days dealing with churches, great and small. In 1937, being on the Parochial Church Council of the St. Albans Cathedral (now the Cathedral Council) he was looked to to devise something better than the method then existing, which consisted of coke stoves standing on the floor, with thin iron flue pipes carried right up the walls. Not only were these quite inadequate for warming the air in any weather below about 45°F, but the smoke condensing in the uprising flues allowed tarry compounds to escape through the joints and disfigure the walls; furthermore the escape of sulphurous gases deteriorated the mediaeval plaster and stonework, so that all-in-all the system seemed to function more in destroying the cathedral rather than in warming it. Kell and Faber studied the matter together, and a fresh system was designed involving radiators and pipes served from gravity-feed type boilers housed underground in the Dean's garden, the whole being subject to complete thermostatic control. This system consumed little more coke than did the original stoves, yet it warmed the cathedral uniformly and adequately to about 60°F in the worst weather conditions. The work was completed prior to the war.

Following this, in 1945, came the appointment for heating Canterbury Cathedral, blitzed during the war. Faber struck up a friendship with Dr. Hewlett Johnson, the 'Red Dean', whose brilliance Faber greatly appreciated – a doctor three times – of Science, Literature and Divinity; and together the two would get into stimulating philosphical discussions. Then in 1948 came the up-dating of the heating of St. Paul's Cathedral in London; and later, following Faber's death, Kell was to deal with the heating of many other cathedrals, including notably Chester and Durham.

There is no doubt that by 1948 the prospects for the firm, so bleak in the immediate post-war days, now appeared back in robust health once more. The staff at Grays Inn had grown to about fourteen – equally balanced between structural and M & E engineers – and was handling the Royal College of Surgeons job as well as a number of commercial buildings overseas, largely in Tanganyika; whilst in the three houses at St. Albans Faber with the bulk of his colleagues ran a team of about thirty, dealing with the other parts of the firm's work-load. So in the remarkably short period of three years, Faber had re-established a working machine of total size similar to his pre-war Romney House set-up, well loaded with work covering much the same range of activities as hitherto.

But now, if he were to succeed in holding the firm together, some form of recognition of his senior assistants as principals could be delayed no longer. Faber's autocratic ways had become unbearable (if faintly amusing), but worse, were proving ineffective and counter-productive: furthermore his grip on events in some areas was already showing signs of slipping, and he was able to realise the bottleneck it would cause to such a complex technical professional team if all major matters had to continue passing through his one pair of hands, now less deft, as sole principal. In 1948, when relationships between clients and their professional advisers and contractors was based more on human patience, trust and cooperation than is the case with today's mood of insurance claims and litigation as a first remedy, Partnership was the natural form of association for Faber to have adopted. Besides, in the professional scene of that time, anything different would have been most unusual.

Faber wanted to take five of his assistants into Partnership. His method of doing this was to draw up his own proposals in great detail, and have these prepared by solicitors Linklaters & Paines into a draft deed for consideration by the other five. On the face of it, his proposals had the appearance of being most generous. Over a period of seven years, his new partners would, on sliding scales, reach a position where they would received virtually half the firm's profits shared equally between them, i.e. ten per cent each. In return for this Faber was asking them to put in no capital; indeed any backlog of fees arising from work-in-progress would be regarded as income of the new Partnership. Had the five been fresh people coming into the firm from outside, this certainly would have been extremely generous; but of course Faber was dealing here with the very men who had done such a great deal over the years before to help build up the firm and indeed support Faber himself.

On closer examination, the draft deed showed Faber as giving very little away, but actually consolidating his own position with the others. Without enumerating here all the details of this somewhat dictatorial deed, Faber, up to whatever age he chose to retire (not exceeding eighty), was to recieve $50\frac{1}{2}$ per cent of the profits. He reserved for himself the right to be the only partner to sign cheques and to engage or dismiss stafff or settle their remuneration; and on a number of points Faber was to be able to terminate forthwith the partnership of any of the others, 'on all of which points the decision of Dr. Faber shall be conclusive'. Of course much of the extremism of this had to be smoothed over by discussion, and subsequently was greatly softened in practice. Obviously the task of signing cheques had to be shared, as also the unenviable and time-consuming business of interviewing staff and assessing their values. But it is true to say that by this time the name Oscar Faber was widely known to stand for engineering excellence and the highest level of integrity, and accordingly was recognisable as a passport that would open doors in any part of the world for any engineer who was to have the privilege of being its bearer. This is till true today; and this was Faber's strength in reaching the agreement he did with his new partners in 1948.

Although the deed wisely stated that goodwill should not be treated as an asset of the partnership for any purpose whatever, Faber could not resist putting in a sentence which attached the goodwill of the *name* of the firm to himself (even after his proposed retirement). Following his death eight years later, the Estate Duty Office was swift to seize on this sentence – and it took the five surviving partners three years to demonstrate and establish that the goodwill had in fact long since been vested in themselves, in that the practice continued to progress on an increasing scale despite the sorrow of Faber's death. Had this not been so, the burden of Death Duty payment might have bankrupted the practice and brought it to an end.

The first reaction to the draft deed came from Monty, who asked whether, if an incoming partner contributed capital, he might then be entitled to a greater share of the profit. This was not on, for a number of reasons; but the two most obvious were firstly that it would cut across Faber's intention of retaining $50\frac{1}{2}$ per cent for himself, and secondly because at that stage the firm was not running on capital at all, but on a control of cash flow. Faber always liked to keep a sizeable sum lying in the bank waiting ready to meet the outgoings of many months to come. The fixed assets were no more than trestle tables in rough condition carrying basic drawing boards propped up at the back on bricks, some second-hand plan-presses on which you hurt yourself trying to open the drawers and close them, some wonderful old typewriters any museum might well have been interested in, and two archaic machines for printing drawings using hung arc-lamps moved horizontally by weights and pulleys kept slow by propeller-type vane governors – all these together stood at no more than a thousand pounds. Not surprisingly, Monty's proposal produced a deal of rankling in the hearts of the others.

Because of the absence of capital, as Faber had it expressed, Vaughan – who was considerably older than the other four of us – wanted some definitive statement in the deed as to provision for Partners, other than Faber, after retirement at the prescribed age of sixty-five. (Faber's income up to the age of eighty was already clearly laid down.) Sorting this out caused extended battles with raised voices between Faber and Vaughan, which in the end Vaughan won. It was the only significant change to the deed that was eventually to be signed; and it sealed, for Faber, the depth of the difference between himself and Vaughan.

And so it came about that on the afternoon of Friday 19th March 1948, Oscar Faber, Jim Vaughan, Rob Kell, K. Montgomery-Smith, Bob Glover and myself gathered at Church Crescent in St. Albans to sign the Deed of Partnership. Actually what was signed were the copies of the final draft, on which the word 'Draft' was scored out; proper engrossed documents were never prepared. The weather that afternoon was dull, and my father saw to it the mood was dull too. Quite genuinely he felt he was letting go something he might well, with advantage, have clung on to much longer as his own. On top of this he was greatly irritated by Monty's approach, and exasperated that Vaughan had won his point about retirement provision. Seated on his own, one side of a large table, he signed all six copies of the deed over sixpenny stamps, passed one to each of the other five, asking them to sign. The deeds were then passed round the table – musical-chairs fashion – each partner adding his signature at every stop, so on completion of the circuit everyone had a deed with six signatures on it. There were no witnesses, and the signatures were of course in an entirely random order, Vaughan was distressed to find the copy he had ended up with had his signature at the very bottom, nowhere near Faber's; and as an appeasement, I made a swap so as to put poor Vaughan's mind at peace.

Kell, always the most self-assured of the five, had thought to add some charm to the occasion by bringing in a little basket containing a bottle of sherry and six glasses wrapped in a napkin. These he had concealed discreetly under the table. But now, the signing over, he lifted the basket onto the table, whereupon Faber expressed his grumpy mood with a loud sigh of exasperation: thus Kell's spirited gesture was rather chilled as glasses were raised and Faber scowled round at each of us in turn. Vaughan and Monty unwisely made nervous little speeches, being allowed time for about a sentence each. Glover and I recognised this was a time it was better to stay quiet. The sherry glasses were quickly packed away, and everyone was hustled off to get back to their work.

The question now was whether the change from the old established style of Dr. Oscar Faber as sole proprietor, to the team of six under the new style of Oscar Faber & Partners, would make for enhanced strength by virtue of numbers, or weakness as a result of the dilution of authority. The first signal would of course be the reaction from outside – whether the intake of fresh jobs would be sustained; and it was not long before it became clear a steady stream of fresh sizeable projects was pouring in. Indeed it was only a few weeks after the deed-signing ceremony that the firm received the appointment for the whole of the civil engineering work for the new Shoreham Cement Works. Entry into this field of operation was going to have a major influence on much of the firm's future.

For over eighty years cement had been manufactured in a small plant at Beeding, near Shoreham-by-Sea on the South Downs of Sussex, on a site lying between the Shoreham-Steyning road and the River Adur. After the Second World War, the British Portland Cement Manufacturers Limited (the BPCM), who operated the Beeding Works, decided to increase very considerably their scale of activities in this area. For Faber, such an involvement with the cement industry was as a return to the womb. The BPCM and the APCM had for years been two large separate groups of cement manufacturers, but in 1926 they had merged becoming the amalgamation of about sixty companies controlled by one interlocking board, the Associated and British Portland Cement Manufacturers Association, generally and more loosely known thereafter as the APCM, though strictly the BPCM was not finally absorbed into the APCM until 1960.

General Critchley had been an active member of both the APCM and BPCM Boards from 1923, and so remained until his death in 1963. One of Critchley's early responsibilities was Publicity; and it was in this capacity that he brought together under one umbrella the various products of the sixty companies by the simple expedient of a common logo – the Blue Circle – blue happening to be the colour of the crayon Critchley had in his pocket at the moment his Board colleagues asked him to sketch on his pad the sort of symbol he had in mind. The yellow lorries with their blue circle were the first joint advertising campaign put across by the APCM's new sales organisation, the Cement Marketing Company, and these vehicles have now been a familiar sight on British roads for sixty years. Little could Critchley have imagined in 1926 this great company would change its name in 1978 to Blue Circle Industries Limited.

Shoreham was to be Blue Circle's first new post-war works, and probably also the first new works in Europe. It was laid out largely in the quarry 1,000ft by 800ft formed by the chalk excavations of the old Beeding Works, and on the opposite side of the Shoreham-Steyning road. Shoreham is a wet-process plant of 400,000 annual tonnage nominal capacity, the process of manufacture consisting essentially of calcining at about 2800°F a slurry mixture of finely divided chalk and clay, and then grinding the resulting clinker into cement. The chalk for the new works is won from benches cut into the Downs above and beyond the cliffs of the old quarry face which stand some 180ft high; and the clay comes from a field at Horton, 2½ miles away, and is pumped as a slurry from Horton to Shoreham in two 8-in. steel pipelines. Shoreham Works has twin horizontal rotary kilns 350ft long and 10ft diameter discharging their gases up a single chimney 300ft high. This chimney was designed in accordance with the theory Faber had developed forty years before, working with Percy Taylor, his old boss and mentor at the APCM. The total effort in designing and administering the whole of the civil engineering work for Shoreham had to be divided equally between the firm's two offices at St. Albans and Grays Inn.

At roughly the same time came also the appointment from the APCM for the installation of the No. 5 kiln at their large works at Hope in Derbyshire. This included a new chimney 400ft high to take the flues from all five of the Hope kilns. Hope Works in 1948 was a wet-process plant, the raw materials being limestone and shale. The limestone comes from a quarry up in the hill high above the Works; and with the installation of the No. 5 kiln, much larger and more modern facilities were required for the primary crushing of this very hard rock. The plant was to be housed in a great hall 115ft high and extending back 100ft behind the vertical face of the cliff formed by the old quarry workings. The powerful crushing machinery was to break down limestone boulders the size of pianos into knobs only a few inches across; and the impact and vibrating forces from this operation necessitated the provision of foundations of enormous mass. At various levels up the building, galleries and other supports had to be provided to suit the needs of the heavy hoppers and chutes; and above all this, and just beneath the level of the roof, a heavy-duty overhead travelling-crane ran the length of the hall, having mastery over the installation and maintenance of the whole equipment.

Also at the time of Shoreham and Hope came appointments from the APCM to design extensions to their works at Lichtenburg in South Africa, at Tolteca in Mexico, and in New South Wales in Australia. In the UK there were to be extensions too, to the works' at Cambridge and Magheramorne; and a new cement-grinding plant was to be constructed at Widnes, and a new distribution depot at Hurlingham on the Thames in London. All these projects added up to a tremendous initiation for the firm into the basic and ever-expanding worldwide cement industry. Their value into the fifties' period was considerable. Through the sixties, work for the cement industry was to account for a considerable part of the firm's growth and development.

Parallel with the great boost the cement industry was giving to the civil section of the new Oscar Faber & Partners, the appointment in 1949 for the Altragelvin Hospital at Londonderry marked the start of a fresh stream of hospital appointments making use particularly of the firm's comprehensive mechanical and electrical experience, and often involving the structural sections as well. The architects for Londonderry were Yorke Rosenberg & Mardall. F.R.S.Yorke and Kell had been friends from the time when Yorke was editor of the technical annual *Specification*, for which Kell every year used to write the chapter on heating and ventilation;

and arising from this association the two had teamed up on a number of school and college jobs, and so a working relationship had developed.

Londonderry was the first new hospital to be built in the UK after the war. In its train were to come the appointments for the rebuilding of the Belfast City Hospital, the rebuilding of parts of the London Hospital, the new Queen Elizabeth Hospital in Aden, and the proposed Kharkh Hospital in Baghdad – though following the revolution in 1958 this appointment, after four years work, was terminated. At the same time, a programme of university work was going through the office, starting in 1949 with Leeds University and the Gold Coast University, followed by the Queens University Belfast in 1951, then Durham, and Liverpool, and Kings College in the Strand, and others to follow.

A number of water-storage structures were also starting to appear in the office. In East Anglia there were water-towers for Thwaite and Yelverton in Norfolk, to be followed in the early sixties by others in Norfolk of rather more modern architectural form at Easton, East Carlton and Swaffham; and over a similar period there were four service reservoirs for the Cambridge Waterworks Company and another at Bedford. Service reservoirs were also designed at this time for Tamale, Dallong, Swedru and Accra in the Gold Coast. There was no doubt that within only a few years of the inception of Oscar Faber & Partners, the firm was entering a period of major and healthy growth.

It was at this time the appointment was received for the Corporation of Lloyd's Building in Lime Street in the City. The architect was T. E. Heysham of the late Sir Edwin Cooper's practice. This was yet another example of the firm providing a total engineering service in challenging circumstances. The post-war restrictions on the construction industry were still making life very difficult; and whereas special waivers had been granted in the case of the House of Commons, such help was not to be made available at Lloyds. As a result of this, 'work permit' limitations caused the construction of the building to be considered as though it were in five separate sections; and rationing and difficulty in procuring steel reinforcements meant that parts of the foundation works which extended through two levels of basement to about 40ft below street level had to be designed and built in mass concrete since otherwise sensible progress could not have been maintained.

Lloyd's is the hub of the insurance world, with international connections, largely the result of its marine department. The origins of this great Corporation go back to the 1680's when the insurers used to meet in a coffee tavern in the City owned by one Edward Lloyd. In 1691 Lloyd moved the business to 16 Lombard

Street, where it continued long after his death until in 1769 a new Lloyd's Coffee House was opened in Popes Head Alley. This latter, however, was found to be so 'inauspicious to health' that a further move had to be made in 1771, this time into part of the Royal Exchange building. By 1923 the Royal Exchange accommodation had become quite inadequate and a site in Leadenhall Street was purchased, where what had become known as Old Lloyd's Building with its large Underwriting Room was opened by King George V in 1928. Even these premises were soon to become overcrowded and the next-door premises, Royal Mail House, were acquired in 1936 to ease the situation.

The foundation stone of the New Lloyd's Building the firm engineered was laid in 1952 by Queen Elizabeth II, and the completed building opened by the Queen Mother in 1957. This new building was linked to the old by means of a tunnel under Lime Street, and by a bridge at first-floor level. It stands generally six stories high above street level, comprises a structural steel frame with *in situ* concrete floors and stairs, and its environmental services include power supply, lighting, twenty-five lifts, water supply, heating, air-conditioning, fire-fighting services, calling systems, and the like. Worthy of special mention is the new Underwriting Room, probably the greatest single space in the City at that time, being 340ft long, 130ft wide, and 38ft high, containing a gallery floor all round at mezzanine level averaging about 40ft width. This room had an air-conditioning system designed to achieve ideal atmospheric working conditions under any circumstances, whether the Room be occupied sparsely, or crowded by any number of persons up to 5000. So satisfactory did the system prove to be, that in the hottest summer weather it was found many people at lunchtime preferred to stay in the building rather than go out into the relative stuffiness of the City streets.

In 1949 the increase in the firm's M & E work had caused the Services Section at Grays Inn to overflow into additional accommodation over a garage in Ampton Street on the other side of Grays Inn Road; but by 1951 even this proved still to be inadequate, and after much searching a rather fine old four-storey building was found at 29 Queen Anne Street, W.1. Here Kell gathered the whole of the M & E Section of the firm, leaving more space at Grays Inn and St. Albans for the Civil and Structural staff. Meanwhile at St. Albans, the City Council was becoming increasingly restless at the three little houses at Worley Road and Church Crescent being used as offices when local housing needs had become so pressing; and in 1955 the houses were given up, and a move made to the relatively grand and spacious building at the bottom of Holywell Hill known as Torrington House, hitherto used as a boarding house for the St. Albans Boys School. So now there was ample space for all the firm's staff in London and St. Albans, and plenty of margin it seemed for future growth.

However it was not to remain so for long: by the early sixties Queen Anne Street and Torrington House were both to be bursting at the seams, and overflow accommodation found in London at Welbeck Street, and in St. Albans at Belmont Hill. Meanwhile branch offices would be set up in Belfast and Cumbernauld near Glasgow, both containing about 20 staff. From the formation of the Partnership in 1948, the firm, over a period of about fifteen years, would grow in strength from 50 to something over 200.

It was during the last ten years of his life, and after the formation of the Partnership, that Faber did most of his overseas travelling. Shortly after the War he was one of a panel of engineers visiting Germany to study what advances had been made there over the war period. This was followed by a series of visits to what was then Tanganyika (now Tanzania) where he gained appointments for several projects with the Nairobi firm of architects Blackburne and Norburn, the largest of which was the abbatoir at Dar es Salaam for Tanganyika Packers Ltd. - an offshoot of Liebigs. Meanwhile, through his associations with Taylor Woodrow, he became involved in the Gold Coast (now Ghana) where he designed a number of stores and office buildings for the United Africa Company including at Accra, Kumasi and Kano, which in turn led him to the appointment for the University of the Gold Coast (later Ghana University) working with architects Harrison Barnes & Hubbard.

In 1951 he fitted in a trip to Australia to examine and report on a site where British Celanese were considering establishing an extensive plant. The Australian trip was taken relatively leisurely - six weeks in all - and coincided happily with the period when his knack of water-colour sketching had reached its peak. Somehow he managed to catch the gum trees, the skies and the Dandenong Mountains of Victoria just as they really are. The calls of the kookaburras and the bell-birds seem almost to ring out of these pictures.

Also in 1951 there was the Northern Ireland Public Enquiry into the tragic collapse of the gangway on the whale factory ship *Juan Peron* when she was lying alongside the quay in the Musgrave Channel at Belfast. A tribunal was set up comprising Oscar Faber to hold a factual investigation, and Herbert Andrew McVeigh KC to act as assessor. The stepped gangway, about 27ft long, had been set at an angle of 45 degrees between cantilever platforms from the ship at levels approximately 38ft and 20ft above quay level; and at the time of the collapse about sixty-five men working on the construction of the ship had been queueing on this gangway in readiness for leaving at the end of their working day. Of these men, eighteen had been killed by the collapse, and forty-one seriously injured. Altogether fourteen learned Counsel attended the Enquiry, as did seventeen witnesses including technical experts. The chairing of a gathering of this calibre and significance – holding a sensible path between relevance and time-wasting – was very much Faber's forte. The collapse had occurred on 31 January; yet the investigation was conducted on 26, 27 and 28 February, and the Report was prepared by 9th March. Sometimes formal committees have been known to take months or more preparing reports of such events.

Following his return from Australia Faber made many journeys to Baghdad over an early scheme for the Khark Hospital with PWD architect Naman Jalili; also to Aden on an appointment from the Crown Agents for the Colonies (as they were then known) for the Queen Elizabeth Hospital, again working in cooperation with Harrison Barnes & Hubbard. Faber always enjoyed taking the lead in every overseas venture, picking up the local slants and seeking to fit in with such customs. Aden was no exception. He came back to St. Albans with a sketch he had made of the method by which the patients in the old hospital were fed, being some sort of mixture prepared in a simple earthenware pot which all the visiting family and aunts and uncles and relations would come and squat in the corridor and heat up over a charcoal burner. He wanted an electric stove designed in the office that would serve the same purpose. It was all so simple and amusing that no one could take it seriously – yet for a while he did.

In 1955, there came the appointment for the whole of the engineering for the Wales Empire Pool in Cardiff. This was to be for the Empire Games in 1958, comprising a swimming pool of international dimensions with diving facilities up to 10 metres. Seating capacity was to be for 2000 for the Games, but when the pool is floored over for boxing or other entertainments, a further 2000 seats can be provided making 4000 in all. This was the first post-war pool of such scale and standard, including in addition to the normal facilities of changing and showering, a comprehensive range of Turkish baths, a Jewish Mikvah bath, and full laundry facilities. At second-floor level are committee rooms, and a restaurant for 200 persons.

It was in the midst of the design stage of the Wales Empire Pool in 1956, that Oscar Faber, on Sunday May 5th, was taken ill. He was working hard in his garden at the time. He died at noon the next morning. The firm's offices in London and St. Albans immediately shut up shop for the rest of the day. The Address by the Dean at the Memorial Service in the Cathedral and Abbey Church of Saint Alban contained the following words:

"Greatly gifted by nature, as fortunate in his personal life as in his work, he might be considered fortunate in his death also. He was ill for one day only. He went out from among us in the plenitude of his powers, before old age or weakness had set their mark on him, stepping out with what might almost apear to be characteristic promptness from the world of activity he so much loved to the peace he knew, that at moments he appeared to seek."

In terms of fresh technical contribution, Faber's death, when he was just short of seventy, really had very little effect on the work being done in the office. However from the point of view of business control, his sudden departure left a rude gap in whatever cohesion his rather unusual methods had been achieving overall. He had always handled the running of the firm himself by the seat of his pants in such a manner that no one else could get a clear view of the total picture, and now, without warning, there was no system and no one groomed in readiness to take over the management of the firm as a whole. All rapport between Faber and Vaughan had ended more than ten years before; and Kell's great strength in his own specialised discipline had caused Faber, over more recent years, to feel somewhat jealous and thrown back on his heels, with the effect, sadly, that he had withdrawn himself from Kell into his own rather lonely shell.

It was over those last years that Faber had come to appreciate more especially the comfort and less pushing nature of Glover. In a tape dictated in 1970, Glover discloses how, after the War, he felt he had become Faber's confidant in the firm, and how Faber had always discussed his engineering and most personal problems with him in private. For years the two of them had gone off daily for lunch *à deux*. Their relationship had reached a point such that, nearer the end, Faber had chosen Glover to be his executor – a function Glover discharged in exemplary fashion. In the closeness of this relationship, Glover felt he had probably seen and understood Faber, in his mellowing years, rather more closely than had any of the others. Glover's last words on this subject were, "The more I knew him, the more I admired his good qualities, and the less I thought of his weaker ones.... It was only when someone tried to put something over on him that he would react violently. That was something I think he would never forgive a person for. ... He was a man who never resented you telling him the truth, even if it was in criticism; but you needed patience to find the opportunity to get him to listen to your point of view – and that might mean waiting quite a time! Then he would thank you for it".

At the time of Faber's death, the five surviving partners were on equal terms. A meeting was convened the following day. The Partnership Deed included provision that the firm should continue

APCM (Blue Circle) first new post-war cement works, at Shoreham, Sussex.

Wales Empire Pool in Cardiff for the 1958 Empire Games.

The Imperial Cancer Research Fund buildings in Lincoln's Inn Fields, London.

Cocoa House, as part of the development at Ibadan, Nigeria.

Hyperbolic-paraboloid concrete roof shells for the main assembly area at Texas Instruments plant at Bedford.

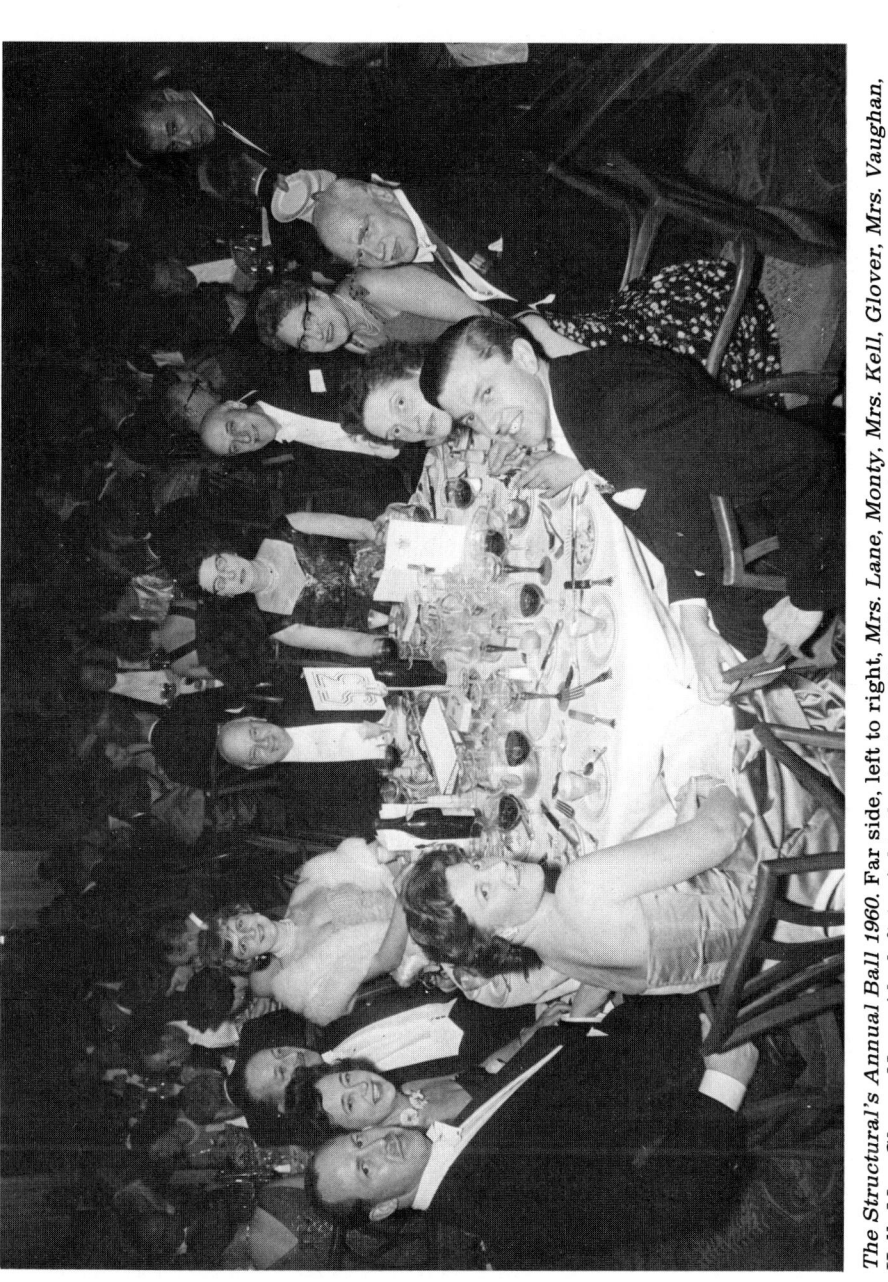

The Structural's Annual Ball 1960. Far side, left to right, Mrs. Lane, Monty, Mrs. Kell, Glover, Mrs. Vaughan, Kell, Mrs. Glover. Near side, left to right, the Author, Miss Montgomery-Smith, P. S. Lane (accountant) now Sir Peter Lane, Mrs. Faber. Vaughan.

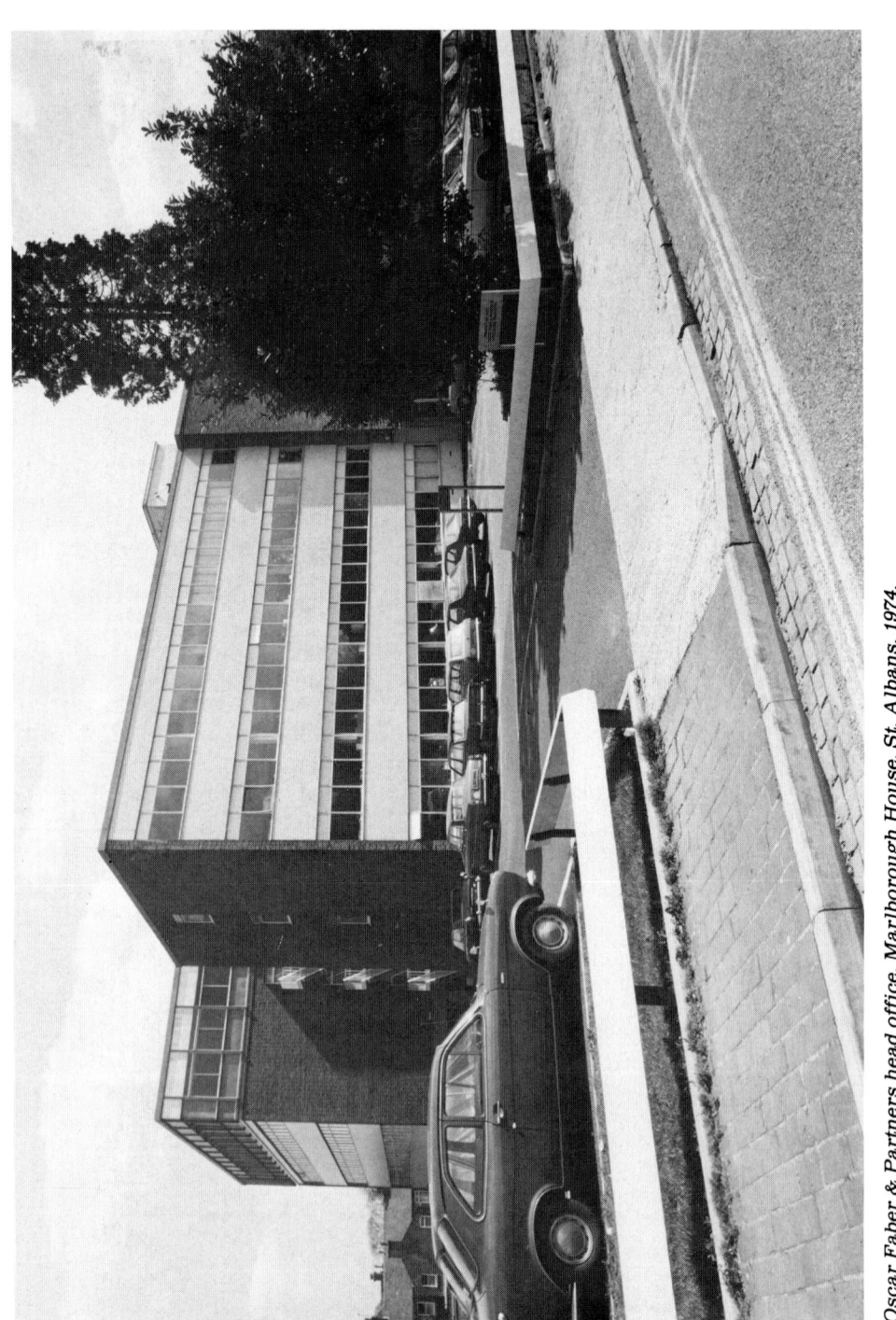

Oscar Faber & Partners head office, Marlborough House, St. Albans, 1974.

Cement works for APCM (Blue Circle) at Hope, in the Derbyshire Peak District.

850-bed Royal Free Hospital at Hampstead Heath, London.

without change; however, there was no definition as to what should happen to all the extraordinary powers that hitherto had been vested in Faber. There were of course other matters more pressing to be dealt with immediately; but unfortunately this had the effect of obscuring the need to appoint someone to fulfil the function that had been Faber's in exercising a central control and sense of leadership. In this respect a void was to remain for a long time to come, the Partners tending to work their own departments separately and pooling the fruits of their efforts, more in the fashion of a Cooperative than a Partnership. In this way the greater total strength that would have been available had there been properly planned coordination was lost.

The one important outcome of the meeting was agreement that Glover should assume responsibility for overall financial control – a role he fulfilled with sober caution and sound success, bearing in mind that Faber had left behind no tangible basis whereby any successor could judge how to plan his course or how to handle his steering. Faber had left no charts, and no one had been allowed a feel of the wheel. Over his first two years, Glover held back from distribution a considerable proportion of the Partners' earnings nett after tax, and in this way for the first time built up recognisable working capital. From then on, the partners' capital accounts figured in the balance sheet, and the finances of the firm stood in more orthodox and business-like form. Glover was to continue controlling the finances, still largely by sense of feel, well into the sixties by which time proper costing and cost-monitoring systems had been running long enough to provide sufficient history for all control to be handled very much more precisely within a fresh and overall management structure.

Glover himself was very much an introvert, never inclined to push too far, and certainly not one with any flair to stand forward and take a lead. Nevertheless, for the next few years he did his best to make up for the inevitable lack of cohesion that arose from absence of leadership, steering the meetings of the partners with some of the skills one recognises in a shrewd company secretary. With no one acting as chairman these meetings tended to wander, often in circles, sometimes almost interminably. It was Glover who made the effort necessary to put this right. He prepared proper agenda for the Partners' Meetings, and produced the first set of minutes; and in 1960 he made the proposal that Vaughan – senior in age and already, incidentally, past retirement age – act as Chairman. Now, at last, there were indications the controlling body of the firm was acquiring some sort of recognisable format.

However, over these years there was the worrying uncertainty of whether the loss of the founder would reflect unfavourably on the well-being of the firm in terms of receipt of fresh appointments and of settled confidence and loyalty amongst the staff. As events turned out it became clear there need never have been any concern on such account. The amount of work coming in continued as before, much of this being to engineering requirements that were increasingly demanding.

In London, for example, a start was to be made on the new Barclays Bank Head Office in Lombard Street. In many respects this was as challenging a task as had been the Bank of England. The Principal Architects were Sir Herbert Baker & Scott with Associated Architects Peter Ednie & Partners. The building has nine floors above street level and rises to a height of 130ft: below the street are three levels of basement, with a 9ft square services tunnel running yet below that. The superstructure frame is of steelwork: and the whole building is air-conditioned by the first high velocity dual-duct system ever designed in this country for a large building.

Also in London came the appointment for the more modern looking English Electric House on the site of the old Gaiety Theatre where Aldwych comes into the Strand opposite Somerset House. The Architects were Adams, Holden & Pearson. The building has eleven floors above the street level, and three levels of basement below. And not so far away, on the south side of Lincoln's Inn Fields, came the appointment for the even more modern building for the Imperial Cancer Research Fund, nine storeys high, again with three levels of basement. The Principal Architects were Young & Hall with Associated Architect John Musgrove. The comprehensive M & E services were designed for extreme flexibility to meet the never-ending changing patterns of research requirements.

Even more flexible were the needs of the piped services at the main Texas Instruments works at Bedford. The Architects for this exciting scheme were O'Neil Ford & Richard Colley of America. The plant included a single-storey manufacturing complex covering an area 400ft square overall, with an 11ft clear-height services basement provided everywhere beneath. When the plant first went into production this basement was packed full of pipes, cables, ducts, and other services. All the concrete floors at Texas Instruments were of special interest, being the first in Europe to be constructed by the lift-slab process. Another structural feature was the use of upswept hyperbolic-paraboloid concrete roof shells, never before designed and built this side of the Atlantic: these were cast as units 50ft square and $2\frac{1}{2}$ ins thick, each supported on only one central column.

Meanwhile a considerable amount of work in West Africa was coming to the firm, some of this being tall modern buildings also requiring innovative methods of design and construction. Two such were Cocoa House in Ibadan, and Western House in Lagos, both in

Nigeria and both by the same imaginative architect Z. Borys of Nickson and Borys & Partners. Also from overseas came the appointment for the Sief Palace in Kuwait. The architect was Pearce Hubbard. This majestic building in yellow brickwork is near the old harbour on a point of land where the Gulf of Kuwait curves away from the Persian Gulf. It is not a residential palace, but the Ruler's place of Government. On the ground floor are the Great Hall which can accommodate 5,000 people, the Assembly Hall and the Sheik's Hall. All these overseas buildings had reinforced-concrete structures and were air-conditioned throughout.

At this time time, too, on the heavier industrial scene, came appointments from the APCM for a new two-kiln cement works at Dunbar in Scotland, with new distribution depots at each of Grangemouth, Dundee, Aberdeen and Inverness. Dunbar was to be the first works in all Scotland to produce cement from the indigenous raw material. These Scottish appointments were the forerunners of numerous others from the APCM including for new works at Cookstown (Ireland) and Weardale, major extensions at Cauldon, Ipswich and Kirton Lindsey, and new distribution depots at Wishaw and Dewsbury.

The Partnership had clearly survived in terms of new work coming in, but now there were signs the administration of the business as a whole was starting to creak at the joints. Things had managed to hold together five years following Faber's death. But what chance was there of this continuing if no positive steps were taken soon?

7

After Oscar Faber's Death

By 1961 it was clear the Partnership needed reconstituting. Vaughan was on his way to sixty-seven and wanting to retire; Kell, Monty and Glover – all with birthdays within a year or so of one another – would be leaving in 1967. Furthermore, up till now, Kell had been the only partner on the M & E side, which, quite apart from burdening the one man unreasonably, had left a sizeable part of the firm too vulnerably disposed. Accordingly a number of well-proved senior members of staff were brought in, these including Cecil Clarke and Arthur Grimes on the Structural side, and Jack Gura on the Services side, who with his greater experience of electrical engineering and modern lift installations formed a desirable complement to Kell's airconditioning and heating expertise.

The problem of goodwill arising from the original 1948 deed was now a thing of the past. Glover took on the task of instructing Linklaters & Paines over the matter of drafting a fresh-style deed. This was a very much more normal document, the basis of which served the Partnership well over the fifteen years to follow. The 1948 deed had dealt with the creation and first growth of Oscar Faber & Partners: the style of the 1961 deed was now to cover a period of succession and metamorphosis, seeing the firm through to its Golden Anniversary in 1971, and beyond. Glover had thought it all out in great depth, very soundly.

If the fifties are to be looked back on as the decade in which the torch of Oscar Faber's entrepreneural genius as sole proprietor was passed down to a group of his long-serving colleagues under the style of Oscar Faber & Partners, the sixties was certainly to be the period in which that fast-grown family team, recognising the dangers of incipient scraggly development, faced up to the need for rationalising itself into a consciously planned organisation with proper management control.

By 1962 it had become clear the continuing absence of overall leadership following Oscar Faber's death in 1956 was allowing too much of the firm's affairs to carry on more by a process of meander, rather than by any train of positive decisions and directives. Some definite action would have to be taken to pull things together if the firm were to stand a chance of coping successfully with the changing nature of operations that might reasonably be anticipated in the years ahead. In fact from 1966 to 1969 the staff size was to increase a further 50 per cent to over 300 in the UK alone, with throughput of work, in real terms, increasing proportionately; and through this period of transformation, the firm's profitability and cash flow were to be maintained consistently at satisfactory levels, all of which is a measure of the cohesion and energy and team-spirit of the partners and staff involved. Inevitably there were pains to be endured; but these were borne generously and cheerfully throughout.

Everything in life is much easier when you know what you're doing. Oscar Faber had always known what he was doing because he had brought the firm along as his own child, fashioning it in accordance with his own desires, restrained only by whatever signals he was picking up from the market place outside and from his assistants within. In his own time, and with a staff never more than 50, this had all worked well enough; but now, with a staff counted in hundreds, and a world becoming increasingly competitive, one could not expect the same 'play it by ear' approach to suffice any longer. This would be as absurd as imagining Dr. W. G. Grace with his natural brilliant flair of a hundred years ago standing up to the highly trained players in the sophisticated test-cricket dramatics we watch and read about today.

Yet still at 1962 the firm had no tangible basis for steering its business affairs, and no conscious policy of where it wished to go or how it thought it might get there. Accordingly I drew up the firm's first long-term programme looking forward a distance of fifteen years. This was agreed by the partners in 1963, and was to be the forerunner of the 2-5-10 year programme prepared in 1964 and thereafter updated annually. Over many years Glover had seen the need for something like this, and although he recognised he was not the man to plan it or put it into effect, he had, in quiet conversations, urged me to start such things and get them moving. Kell, always much more pressed with his involvement and great task in leading the M & E half of the firm, made his contribution by holding himself available for good counsel whenever required, and never stood in the way of what the younger partners were wanting. Right through to their year of retirement (1967) and thereafter as Consultants, both Kell and Glover showed every enthusiasm, encouragement and real support for all the change they knew was going on. Both had developed the qualities of 'elder statesman': both were outstanding in this.

The first thing needing to be done was to set up a simple and effective costing system that would enable detailed analyses to be made of the firm's true profitability. It was important to know which types of project were the more rewarding, which were the crisper outside organisations to work with, which were the departments and teams within the firm adopting techniques achieving the greater decisiveness and throughput, by whom and in what manner the better fee bargains were being struck, and so on. The costing system would provide an understanding of all operation costs in such detail that in future all the firm's business could be planned ahead, not only in terms of meeting technical and professional responsibilities, but also in terms of overall development, improvement, and expansion. This all sounds so basic and obvious today, it hardly seems worth mentioning now as an item of history; yet in fact the introduction of the costing system was the most difficult thing to get agreed and put into operation, since clearly it would lead to individual accountability.

It has to be remembered that in those days the firm was spread between houses in St. Albans, houses in London's West End, chambers in Grays Inn, a house in Belfast and two small houses at Cumbernauld near Glasgow. Many of the staff's working horizons were limited almost to the number of people sharing the domestic-sized rooms they were working in, sometimes only two or three. Furthermore Kell's M & E people, encapsulated in the West End and across the water in Ireland, seemed worlds away from the civil and structural people equally split up as between Grays Inn, St. Albans and Scotland. Not only was this about as illogical and wasteful as one could imagine for a firm whose greatest strength was its special competence in handling the more complex problems of M & E services coordinated within challenging structures: it was also having the effect that in many cases the people in the different offices hardly knew one another. What sort of atmosphere was this in which to persuade people to cooperate for the first time in a fully exposing costing-system; for without cooperation it was clear the system could be sabotaged at least to the extent of losing the very sensitivity needed to achieve the objectives now being sought.

In the earlier days of the firm, when it had been much smaller, the scheme of things had been that the staff, other than the seniors, should get on with the work they were given, keeping their noses down producing sound calculations and good drawings in the least time possible. But in the larger firm of the sixties what was required was to draw on every ounce of imagination, initiative and talent available within the team as a whole; and this meant the closest possible rapport as between partners and staff all the way up and down the line. Whereas time spent in office hours mulling over general matters had hitherto been rather frowned upon, the mood now was one of encouraging people to share and talk out their problems and ideas over coffee and buffet luncheon sessions, and with a beer or a scotch as each day drew towards its close.

To this end regular Discussion Group meetings were introduced. These started as purely internal affairs; but soon outside speakers were brought in, films were shown, and so the mood of communication and togetherness was spread around. At the same time a start was made on the firm's first house magazine. This was published quarterly. The need for a house magazine – not a very usual feature in those days – arose from the size to which the firm had grown and the way it was spread in so many different offices. The truth was that even the partners were having difficulty in keeping track of all the clients and architects the firm was working with scattered about the country and overseas as well.

It was in 1964 the firm's first Annual Report was produced. The new costing and bookkeeping systems had only been in operation for one year, so there was still a shortage of detailed cost history. Certain of the figures in the Report were therefore necessarily inexact. Nevertheless sufficient hard information was already coming through to enable fundamental trends to be recognised, defined, and commented upon. Once the facts can speak for themselves, opinions and arguments can be much reduced. Various elements of guesswork could now be done away with, and the facts made use of to determine the direction the firm should be moving and the rate at which it should be doing this. The Annual Reports in years to follow were of course based on fuller information, and could for this reason be increasingly specific and more thrusting.

The same year happened by good chance to be the twenty-fifth anniversary of the firm's first arrival in St. Albans in 1939, and advantage was taken of this to throw a celebration Dinner Party and Dance at the Waterend Barn as a launch for the Christmas holiday. (This was the start of the now annual Christmas dinner-dance parties.) Long tables were laid out in banquet style with a printed table plan, each table being hosted by a partner seated at its centre. Every lady on arrival was presented with a posy – their men decked in dinner jackets. Aperitifs flowed freely until the announcement of dinner which proved to be a grand and festive affair with pleasant wines. Toasts were called across the room from table to table with much lively banter. Altogether two hundred and sixty attended. Rob Kell made one of his off-the-cuff speeches recalling how things had been in the little St. Albans houses twenty-five years before: how, for economy, rubbers had been issued cut in half (so there were always twice as many wasted ends); pencils had to be used down to about two-inches before new ones could be had; and the coal in the little open grates had been bought so specially cheap and was of such a hard industrial nature, it would neither burn properly nor give off any heat! Having recalled the trials and the fun of the previous twenty-five years, Kell proposed a toast for the success and happiness of the next twenty-five. After the dinner the tables were pushed back, and dancing took the evening through to the early hours.

In 1964 it was laid down that the firm should start making a positive effort to get more and larger jobs overseas. Subsequent programmes went further, giving a clear target that 30 per cent of the firm's output should be in overseas projects, and this is roughly what it built up to. To help achieve this the firm's first brochure was prepared. Apart from its first few pages of introduction, each subsequent sheet had on either side a single photo illustrating one job together with a 20-word caption. From this, a potential client could grasp, within a minute or two, the firm's involvement in about fifty selected projects. For its time, this document – in simple black and white – gave a suitable crisp and effective image. Today, of course, the use of brochures has been developed to become a standard tool for all the construction professions, and copy-writers and graphics designers are used to good effect: but in the sixties such matters had to be handled with less sophistication and rather more caution and modesty.

Now it was necessary to get the firm out of its unsuitable domestic scale buildings and into proper modern accommodation with all the benefits of open-plan layout. Furthermore the arrangement of M & E people being situated entirely separately from civil and structural people could not be left to continue any longer; and I was absolutely determined a staff of all disciplines totalling about 300 should eventually be gathered together in one fine building somewhere in St. Albans which would then be the firm's Headquarters. Much of the inspiration for this came from my P.A. at the time – Frank Metcalfe. The St. Albans building was a remarkable projection of imagination, when one realises the firm's total staff of 200 was then split as between London and St. Albans in the ratio of 3 to 1. Furthermore the provision of parking for more than 100 cars was way outside the norm of its time.

It was realised the attainment of such a target would be achieved only with considerable difficulty. The sums of money involved were to be out of all proportion to the rent figures the firm had been faced with hitherto. At the early sixties many of the staff were living in London, and south of the river, and it was doubtful how many of these would be willing to uproot themselves and face the problems of finding fresh homes, schools and so on in Hertfordshire. Nor was it clear whether clients would be pleased to have their consulting engineers removed from London and out – as it seemed – to the sticks. And would there be a sufficient catchment area handy to St.

Albans to provide the build-up of staff numbers the new programmes were then envisaging?

The crunch came when two fine Victorian houses side by side at Nos. 16 and 18 Upper Marlborough Road were put on the market for auction. It was thought these together would cost about £35,000, as indeed proved to be the case. The two gardens would provide a site of 100ft total frontage by 250ft depth. It could be a rare opportunity to make a start on the venture. Momentarily it drew the older partners up in their tracks: it was the first realisation ever to strike the partnership table of a capital commitment of such scale. After forty years of the older style of accommodation and relatively crude office equipment, it must have been difficult for the older men to appreciate the significance of the change they were being asked to come along with. Indeed at that stage the firm's proposed costing system was only in embryo stage: no one had any real knowledge of what financial strength there was to back the idea; and it had to be admitted the proposal was, to say the least, something of a calculated risk. Kell with his charming smile asked whether I could kindly explain to him the difference between a 'calculated risk' and an 'outright gamble'. I could not! The whole matter was chewed over for some time with care and sincerity, and eventually agreement reached in good heart that the development should proceed.

It was obvious things would have to be taken in cautious stages, partly because of the risk or 'gamble' involved, partly to enable the movement of staff from London – and termination of the leases there – to be handled without disruption to work or too much inconvenience to staff, and partly to suit the time scale of expansion that had been planned. In the event, the building was constructed in three phases, each of units 80ft long and 40ft wide, and each having four floors of office accommodation. Phase I was completed in 1965, and Phase II in 1968. Later the same year, quite out of the blue, the adjacent house up the road at No. 20 was offered for private sale, and promptly bought for £12,000, enabling Phase III to be completed in 1974. This was formally opened in May by Dick Harrison – then Senior Partner of another firm, and Chairman of the Association of Consulting Engineers.

When one looks back now, 1968 stands out as the year by which proper office accommodation had achieved its full impact on morale and attitude right across the firm. In that year the bulk of the M & E and structural people from London were able to move into Upper Marlborough Road, giving at last a fine sense of unity, strength and quiet comfort – the wear and tear of commuting to and from London was thankfully a thing of the past. By then also the Scottish office had moved into a new open-plan building in the centre of Glasow; and at the same time the firm was settling itself into a new open-plan block in the centre of Manchester. Only the

Belfast office continued in domestic-scale accommodation, and this was because an eventual withdrawal from Ireland was already anticipated. Whereas in 1965 the whole firm had been working in buildings aged a hundred years or more, in three years nearly all had been moved into offices none of which was more than three years old.

At this time too the firm's information department was created. A new Barbour Index of manufacturers' catalogues was installed. The firm joined HERTIS – the Herts C.C. Technical Library and Information Service – based at Hatfield College (now Hatfield Polytechnic): this coordinates the information and resources of all the Hertfordshire colleges, thereby providing access to all these libraries and services for information and research, as well as the use of the Colleges' Laboratories. The information department quickly built up to a staff of five, with a total shelving capacity of a thousand feet. Unlike a library, where normally the main emphasis is on books, much of the holdings comprise journals and reports from research and professional associations and Government departments.

The mood of the firm was ripe now for formalising a Sports & Social Club. Every member of staff was welcomed in, so that funds could be gathered sufficient to support varied and ambitious events. A committee was formed including a chairman, secretary, auditor and others; rules for the club were drawn up and published; and a president and vice-presidents were chosen. Funding was by subscriptions from members, plus whatever more could be got from raffles and other legal lotteries – to become a source of much fun at the firm's annual Christmas dinner-dance – and whatever sum all this might produce, the partners undertook to double out of their own resources. The firm's Golden Anniversary party was to be the opportunity taken to inaugurate the annual presentation of the President's Trophy – a fine silver bowl – to a member of the Club considered by the committee and the president to have contributed outstandingly to the Club's success and well-being.

There can be little doubt the most far-reaching technical stride taken by the firm in the sixties period was its entry into the field of computer science: from there, so many other doorways were to be opened. From early on, Glover had been watching the increasing uses to which the digital computer could be put, and was clear that any firm ignoring the progress then being made would be running the risk of falling behind over the whole spectrum of its consultancy and business affairs. It was Glover who first suggested getting involved with an outside computer bureau. From this point on it became pretty clear anything less than having ones own in-house machine would fall short of the real need: no one can ever feel wholly at ease in computer work without having a machine available close at hand, to see and touch and play with. Nevertheless even in the sixties period there were still seniors in the firm who would argue at length that such a step was unjustifiable, and the great cost quite unnecessary. Looking back, one recognises this as an interesting measure of the rate at which our technological age has been advancing and peoples minds had to adjust to keep pace. Soon the firm's first computer member of staff was taken on for setting up and running the new Computer Department, an IBM 1130 machine was installed and thereafter operated generally on an open job-shop basis, offering engineers the opportunity to operate the machine themselves whenever they so wished, though members of the new computer staff were available always to help as much or as little as might be required. In this way any preconceived shyness or sense of mystery about the new toy was quickly dispelled. The early success of the Faber computer programs led almost immediately to requests from outside firms – consulting engineers and contractors – to hire time on the IBM machine so as to have use of the programs. A separate company – Faber Computer Operations Limited – was formed in 1971.

Although the present chapter is intended mainly to be about changes of organisation, administration and attitudes within the firm, one can hardly let the whole of the sixties go by without making brief mention of just a few of the jobs being undertaken at that time. These included the 850-bed Royal Free Hospital which now stands on a fifteen-acre site overlooking Hampstead Heath: it comprises a nine-storey ward tower, cruciform in plan, rising above a six-storey podium containing patient diagnosis and treatment areas, and a five-storey podium containing the administration and research departments. The architects for the hospital were Watkins Gray Woodgate International. The M & E services include full air-conditioning in the tower block and to internal areas of the podia using a dual-duct high-velocity system. A vertical transport system, designed to cut walking distance to a minimum, is provided by 24 high-speed lifts. The LEB supply is at 11 kV, and terminates at a switchboard with facilities for switching between incoming feeders in the event of loss of supply on any feeder; and an 11 kV ring distribution system connects between all load centres in the hospital.

Through this same period, the civil side of the firm handled many more cement projects. The two most challenging were the doubling in output and conversion of APCM's Hope Works in Derbyshire from wet-process to a 1.2 million ton per annum semi-dry works; and a shared involvement with the APCM's Central Engineering Civil Department in the construction of their new 3.5 million ton per annum wet-process works at Northfleet in Kent, the largest cement works to be built in the world up to that time.

Also there came the appointment to work with Hubbard Ford & Partners for the Property Services Agency of the Department of the Environment on the new international telephone exchange on the north bank of the Thames next to Cannon Street railway station. This was Europe's biggest such exchange, and one of the largest of its kind in the world. Appropriately known as Mondial House, it has a total of twelve floors. The 2½ levels of basement construction 330ft by 180ft involved a concrete raft foundation 50ft below high-tide level immediately behind the old river wall, in consequence of which there were problems of high water pressure and risk of flotation in both the temporary and permanent conditions: this was dealt with by a pressure-relief drainage system built under the raft. The main electricity supplies at 11 kV are taken directly to the chief load centres; standby equipment in major plant centres is backed by six standby diesel generating sets in the lower basement. Electrical energy fed to the Post Office switching apparatus culminates naturally in heat as much as 25 watts per sq. ft. of floor space – the equivalent of a kilowatt electric fire for every area 6ft x 6ft – necessitating cooling which is provided by four hermetic centrifugal compressor sets having a total capacity of 4,400 tons of refrigeration.

And so, in 1971, Oscar Faber's firm reached it's Golden Anniversary. In November the *Consulting Engineer* published an extensive review of the firm's growth and status under the title 'Fifty Years and Still Young'. This concluded with the paragraphs as here:

> "Oscar Faber & Partners have grown to their present size for two main reasons. In the first place their comprehensive service leads them to the larger jobs, and they need the capacity to handle these with some reasonable hope of continuity of workload. In the second place they would not otherwise be able to afford to run their own computer, their own information service and a variety of other back-up facilities if they were smaller; nor would they be able to enjoy a sports and social club, and provide the high level of working comforts and conditions for their staff.
>
> "Now they have mastered the problem of generation succession they feel that with 50 years behind them they are poised and well prepared to face the more challenging years ahead. They are watching very closely the changes in attitudes towards the consulting engineer within and without the industry. The firm is so attuned to meet the client's needs it is

certain that as future demands change, Oscar Faber & Partners will be there to meet them."

The same month a dinner dance celebration party was held in the Dorchester Hotel ballroom. This was attended by nearly six hundred guests who included clients, architects, quantity surveyors, other consulting engineers, contractors, and members of staff - all with their ladies. All were good friends of the firm over the years - a few going back to the early days of the twenties. Of course Rob Kell and Bob Glover were there. So also was Sir Frederick Snow, whose first contact with the firm had been at Northolt Park Racecourse in 1927. Oscar Faber and Freddie Snow's paths had crossed on innumerable occasions since that time, and it was fitting Sir Frederick should have been asked to propose the toast of Oscar Faber & Partners. This he did in charming generous terms, linked with reminiscences of happy sparring exchanges with Faber over a period of nearly thirty years. Then there came the dancing which had about it a warm and festive mood. Even to this day there are some who remember the evening as a fitting celebration to mark the firm's good fortune in having come through successfully its first fifty years of professional practice.

For myself, having then completed my function as instigator of the overhaul and refit of the whole firm, and seen it build up its strength and size to more than six times what it had been before the Partnership had been formed, I felt my enthusiam would be likely to diminish if I stayed in the place as an executive much longer. I had had a fair crack of the whip and my partners had been more than patient in allowing me as much rope as they had. We were now a team of a dozen partners and as many associates, and it seemed only fair the others should have a freer hand in making their own decisions and more sense of fun and personal achievement in whatever successes were to follow. Accordingly I gave two years notice of my intention to slither out, during which period I would draw up my last 2-5-10 year programme which I hoped might serve some useful purpose to the others after I had gone. I was confident all was set well in terms of personnel and organisation to run the next ten-year term in good shape; and I was more than happy that my role as Senior Partner would be passed to the capable hands of Jack Gura who, for a long time, had been managing the M & E Services side of the firm, and in later years been in control of all the firm's finances. It was agreed I should continue as a Consultant to the practice over these years and so retain some distant interest; nevertheless I should now have the luxury of more time to spend in writing, in doing my own outside consultancy work, and also doing some practical research work - particularly in the field of silo design. This all worked out very happily.

After these ten years, the firm – then styled as the Oscar Faber Partnership – carried out a reorganisation of its own form, with the result it functioned no longer as a partnership but as an unlimited liability company. Jack was now retired. Such are the changes of time, and probably inevitable. My father could never have envisaged such a thing. Then, after a further five years, everything was changed to limited liability under the flag of Oscar Faber plc: I wonder what the 'Old Man' would have thought of that!